The Complete Guide to
HOUSEPLANTS

The Complete Guide to
HOUSEPLANTS

The Easy Way to Choose and Grow Healthy, Happy Houseplants

Valerie Bradley

Reader's Digest

The Reader's Digest Association, Inc.
Pleasantville, New York/Montreal/Hong Kong

A READER'S DIGEST BOOK
This edition published by the Reader's Digest Association, Inc. by arrangement
with Collins & Brown, 10 Southcombe Street, London W14 0RA, England

FOR COLLINS & BROWN
Project Editors: Marie Clayton, Carly Madden
Designer: Jeremy Tilston

FOR READER'S DIGEST:
U.S. Project Editor: Kim Casey
Canadian Project Editor: Pamela Johnson
Gardening Consultant: Miranda Smith
Copy Editors: Andrea Chesman, Marilyn Knowlton
Designers: Jennifer R. Tokarski, Amanda Wilson
Senior Project Designer: George McKeon
Executive Editor, Trade Publishing: Dolores York
President & Publisher, Trade Publishing:
Harold Clarke

Library of Congress Cataloging-in-Publication Data:
Bradley, Valerie.
The complete guide to houseplants : the easy way to choose and grow healthy,
happy houseplants / Valerie Bradley.
p. cm
ISBN-13: 978-0-7621-0890-9
ISBN-10: 0-7621-0890-8
1. Houseplants. 2. Indoor gardening. I. Title: Complete guide to houseplants. II.
Title: Houseplants. III. Title

SB419.B692 2006
635.9'65- dc22
2005051195

Address any comments about
The Complete Guide to Houseplants to:
    The Reader's Digest Association, Inc.
    Adult Trade Publishing
    Reader's Digest Road
    Pleasantville, NY 10570-7000

For more Reader's Digest products and
information, visit our website:
    www.rd.com (in the United States)
    www.readersdigest.ca (in Canada)
    www.rdasia.com (in Asia)

Printed in China

1 3 5 7 9 10 8 6 4 2

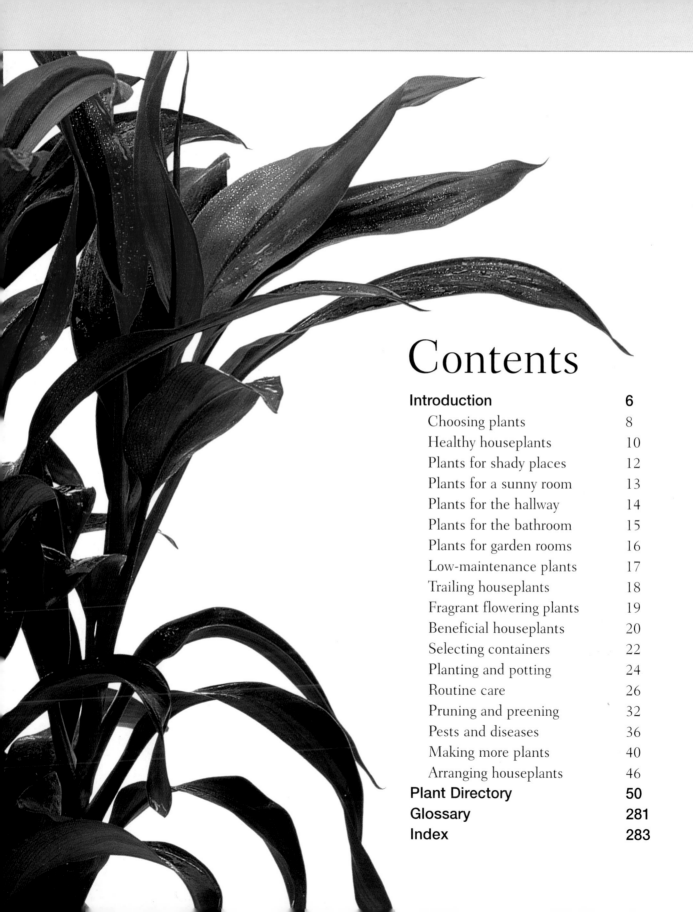

Contents

Introduction

Most of the plants we grow indoors are outdoor plants from warmer climates. They have their origins in jungles and deserts, tropical rain forests and wide-open plains. They have the same needs and requirements in terms of light and watering as the plants we have in our gardens, although they usually have higher requirements for warmth and humidity. Trying to grow a plant in unsuitable conditions has the same result indoors as outdoors—it will become stressed as it tries to cope, it will be vulnerable to pest and disease attack, and it will ultimately give up the struggle and die. Unfortunately, as far as indoor plants are concerned, this happens so often that many people regard them as short-term and expendable.

Take the time to find out where your plant naturally lives. Most houses have a variety of conditions to offer, from a warm, humid kitchen to a cool bedroom. Whether it is bright or dark, warm or cold, it will almost always suit the plants you'll enjoy. In this book, we have tackled each area in turn, giving a list of suggestions for plants in each case. Whether you want a lush foliage plant or a pretty flowering one, something to climb or something to trail gracefully from a hanging basket, there is a plant for all but the most inhospitable situation.

This tender *Rhododendron* 'Lady Alice Fitzwilliam' produces a fantastic show of scented flowers in spring.

After choosing your plant, the next step is to keep it alive and thriving, and the key to success is to take the time to get to know the plants in your care. The directory section of this book is an alphabetical list of popular indoor plants and gives their ideal growing conditions. It also tells you whether a plant needs special treatment and if it is possible to propagate it.

This book will help the beginner start growing houseplants and the more experienced indoor gardener to progress by offering inspiration and explanations. A good understanding of how plants grow healthy and strong will help ensure that your houseplants achieve that goal.

RIGHT: Amaryllis (*Hippeastrum*) is a popular indoor bulb. It produces a magnificent display of glamorous flowers.

BELOW: An exotic display of winter-flowering plants set in a low, decorative pot.

Choosing plants

Any plant, however large or small, whether intended just for the short term or as a permanent addition, is an investment. By doing a little research before you buy, you can save yourself time and money. To thrive, plants must grow in the best environment possible.

Mixed ferns and a creeping fig

A plant for indoors is usually destined for a certain position, whether it be a windowsill, shelf, or table, and the wide range of plants available in the nursery or garden center ensures that there will be a plant to suit almost every situation.

The requirements for light, warmth, humidity, and space vary considerably from plant to plant, and it is worth assessing how much of each is available beforehand. Remember that indoors, the plant has no resources to call on, so you must provide everything it needs or it will die. Give it the right conditions, however, and it will thrive.

What the plant needs

Try to make use of all the different ways in which plants can be displayed: in floor-standing containers, on pedestals, on furniture, against a wall, and hanging from the ceiling or a wall bracket.

Light

Light is essential to a plant in order for the process of photosynthesis to take place. When the chlorophyll within the leaves reacts with light, it produces sugars and starches, which are transported down through the plant. Inadequate levels of light mean that the process slows down and the plant begins to suffer slow growth and a lack of flowers. A prolonged lack of light will result in a pale-colored plant, elongated by its search for light and weak and floppy as a consequence.

Temperature

Every plant has an ideal temperature range in which it prefers to grow and a wider one that it can tolerate. Growing in its ideal range—if all other circumstances, such as moisture, are also adequate—a plant will thrive. It will grow well and happily, producing lush foliage and rich flowers. In the range it can tolerate, growth will be slower, foliage thicker and darker, and flowers smaller or nonexistent. Outside this range, the survival of the plant cannot be guaranteed.

CHECKLIST

- During the growing season, most indoor plants need a temperature between 60–71°F (15–21°C).
- Those from less tropical regions need a cooler site at 50–60°F (10–15°C).
- Young plants and seedlings will grow better in a constant warm temperature between 65–71°F (18–21°C) and away from direct sun.
- Do not site plants directly over sources of heat, such as radiators.
- Keep sensitive plants away from drafty windows and doors.
- Allow plants to have their winter rest period in cooler conditions.
- In winter, plants on the windowsill may get chilled once the curtains are drawn because the temperature near the glass is several degrees lower than inside the room.
- A shaded windowsill facing the sun in summer will be too hot for most leafy plants, and even some succulents.

Humidity

The term "humidity" refers to the amount of water held as vapor in the air. It is measured as a percentage; 0 is totally dry, and 100 is so saturated that the vapor is fog or steam. The amount held varies according to the temperature because warm air can hold more moisture than cold.

All indoor plants, even cacti, need a humidity level between 40 and 60 percent, because that level affects the amount of water the plant loses through the process of transpiration. The warmer and drier the conditions, the more water the plant loses through the leaves. This is especially true when the leaves are thin and papery, although even thick, leathery leaves can suffer in very dry conditions. If the water is not quickly replaced by the roots, the result will be brown tips and edges on the leaves where the cells have died.

How to improve humidity

Raising the humidity means increasing the amount of water contained in the air. You can do this by using a fine misting spray around the plant at least once a day and more often if the temperature is high and by standing individual pots on

The Boston fern (*Nephrolepis exaltata* 'Bostoniensis') is not a deep shade lover, but it does well near an east-facing window.

saucers of pebbles or gravel. By filling the saucer with water, you can let the plant take up what it needs and the rest can evaporate around the leaves. You can also place the terra-cotta pot of a plant such as azalea, which prefers cool, moist, root conditions, inside a larger container with a layer of moist sphagnum moss between the two pots so that the moisture from the moss will evaporate.

Ficus lyrata

Healthy houseplants

The better condition a plant is in when it is purchased, the better its chances of survival. A plant bought at the nursery where it was raised should be in the best possible condition because it will be younger and healthier than those that have had to go through the stress of being transported.

Plants sold on the roadside or at a yard sale are exposed to drying winds; high or low temperatures, depending on the time of year; and pollution. In a supermarket, unless there is a separate area dedicated to the plants, watering might be erratic and the lighting poor. In the garden center, they should be well cared for in terms of watering, although the longer they remain unsold, the more they will begin to suffer as their reserve of slow-release fertilizer runs out.

Selecting a healthy plant

Look for a plant with strong, healthy-looking leaves of a good, vibrant color with no blotches or nibbled edges. The stems should be firm, not floppy, and the growth should be compact—not long and weak, which indicates a period spent in poor light. Choose a plant with most of the flowers still in bud to give the longest flowering period and check the leaves and stems for pests such as scale insects or whitefly. Disease will show itself as gray, furry mold around the base of the plant or as pale blotches on the surfaces of the leaves.

Size is a matter of preference: A small plant will cost less, and although it will soon need repotting, it will adapt quickly to its new surroundings and begin to grow. A larger specimen will have instant impact, although it will cost more and may take longer to adapt to the conditions in its new home.

Plants that are blooming, such as polyanthus, and spring bulbs, have the added attraction that once they have finished flowering, they can be planted outdoors and be enjoyed for years to come.

Rex begonias, with their attractive and varied foliage, do really well displayed together, but away from direct sunlight.

CHECKLIST—THINGS TO LOOK FOR BEFORE BUYING YOUR PLANTS

If a plant shows any signs of the following conditions, it is probably best not to purchase it. There will generally be other choices of the same plant available, and if not, you can always go elsewhere. Following this advice will prevent your plant from suffering other problems very quickly, infecting other houseplants in your home, or failing and dying.

• Weak, pale, spindly growth: This generally indicates that the plant will never grow strongly as it matures.

• A plant that has already finished flowering: The plant is already past its best at the moment you are about to buy it.

• Leaves with blotches, wiggly lines, holes, or nibbled edges: Sure signs of disease and/or pest infestation.

• Insects anywhere on the plant: Do not invite unwanted intruders into your home—they might attack your other plants.

• Curled or twisted new shoots: A plant in this condition will never grow well in the future.

• Oval brown lumps on the stems: Further signs of disease that should be avoided at all costs.

• Gray mold anywhere on the plant: A common affliction that indicates general bad health.

• Soggy, rotting patches anywhere on the stems: A sign of root rot or that the plant is pot-bound.

• Shrunken, withered roots: Without healthy, vibrant roots no plant will ever flourish.

• Smelly or white-encrusted potting soil, or soil that has shrunk away from the sides of the pot: Poor soil leads to unhealthy growth.

Plants for specific locations

Plants would not naturally choose to live indoors, where the air is dry, the growing area is severely restricted, and supplies of water are limited. In fact, it is amazing that some plants survive indoors at all, yet they do. They often survive periods spent in less-than-ideal conditions without suffering too much damage, but they will not thrive as well as they would in a situation perfectly suited to their needs.

What to avoid

The worst places in the house, in plant terms, are in direct heat, deep shade, or strong air currents. Not many plants can tolerate being on a windowsill facing the sun in summer, when the intensity of the heat can boil the water inside the leaf cells and cause them to die.

In deeply shaded parts of the house, light levels are not sufficient to allow photosynthesis to take place, denying the plant the carbohydrates it needs to live. In a drafty position, a lack of humidity will cause the leaves of more delicate plants to turn brown and wilt.

Ease the plant out of its pot to check that the roots are light colored, firm, and free of insect larvae.

Ficus binnendijkii

Plants for shady places

Flowering houseplants do not thrive in the more shady areas of the home because they need maximum light to mature and produce flower buds. For this situation, choose foliage plants with mid to dark green leaves because they can cope with low light.

Keep in mind that nothing will grow where the light level is very low because it will be unable to photosynthesize. Avoid white- or yellow-leaf variegations. The color will be lost as the plant attempts to adapt to the more shady surroundings— there is no chlorophyll in the variegated part of the leaf, reducing the plant's ability to produce food. Look for plants with leathery or waxy dark green leaves. The darker green they are, the better the plant will tolerate the lack of light.

PLANTS FOR SHADY PLACES

Aspidistra elatior CAST-IRON PLANT. Enjoys partial shade and tolerates a wide range of temperatures. Cream and purple flowers are produced in spring but they are barely visible through the foliage.

Asplenium nidus BIRD'S-NEST FERN. Never place in direct sunlight. Keep thoroughly moist.

x Fatshedera lizei IVY TREE. Display in cool light. Variegated forms require more light than completely green ones. Keep moist from spring to autumn.

Ficus binnendykii NARROW-LEAF FIG. Graceful, dropping, pointed-tipped foliage.

Howea forsteriana KENTIA PALM. Tolerant of a wide range of indoor conditions but avoid deep shade. Keep medium moist from spring to autumn.

Maranta leuconeura PRAYER PLANT. Enjoys partial shade in moderate room temperatures.

Monstera deliciosa SWISS CHEESE PLANT. Position where there is indirect sunlight and keep barely moist all year round. Train stem up against a moss pole.

Nephrolepis exaltata 'Bostoniensis' BOSTON FERN. Indirect sunlight or warm partial shade; avoid deep shade. Keep moist at all times in normal room temperature.

Philodendron bipinnatifidum TREE PHILODENDRON. Enjoys indirect sunlight or partial shade. Keep moist from spring to autumn. Do not let medium dry out over winter.

Saxifraga stolonifera MOTHER OF THOUSANDS. This plant needs indirect sunlight or partial shade. Keep in a room where the temperature is cooler than normal.

Schefflera elegantissima FALSE OR FINGER ARALIA. Needs indirect sunlight in a normal room temperature. Keep moist from spring through autumn.

Senecio macroglossus NATAL IVY OR WAX VINE. Fairly tolerant but copes with partial shade well. Keep moist, but give enough water to prevent plant from drying out over winter.

Plants for a sunny room

This would seem to be the ideal spot for most plants, with plenty of light and warmth, but as with any other location, you still need to make sure you are putting the right plant in the right place. Most indoor plants will thrive as long as they are not in direct scorching sun, particularly at midday.

Scented-leaved geraniums

The bright hot sun, intensified by window glass, will cause sap inside the leaf to overheat and damage the cells, leading to scorching. Desert cacti can usually tolerate a sunny windowsill, as do seasonal pot plants when the heat is less intense, such as spring bulbs and flowering plants. Other plants will be happy for most of the day, but may need a little protection when the sun is at its highest.

The *Clivia miniata* has orange, slightly fragrant, bell-shaped flowers.

PLANTS FOR A SUNNY ROOM

Clivia miniata Prefers indirect sunlight. Needs a winter rest period of about 6–8 weeks.

Grevillea robusta Enjoys direct, but not fierce, sunlight.

Hibiscus rosa-sinensis Prefers direct, but not fierce, sunlight.

Jasminum polyanthum Position where there is both indirect and direct sunlight in a cool room.

Mammillaria spp. Enjoys direct sunlight in a warm room.

Nerium oleander Direct sunlight at normal room temperature.

Passiflora caerulea Direct sunlight at normal room temperature.

Pelargonium spp. Enjoys direct or indirect sunlight.

Pentas lanceolata Keep moist and position in direct sunlight.

Plumbago auriculata Needs direct sunlight at normal room temperature. Deadhead flowers to promote new buds.

Rosa chinensis 'Rouletii' Keep in direct sunlight at normal room temperature but provide high humidity.

Sanseveria trifasciata Fairly tolerant; enjoys a position in both direct or indirect sunlight.

Stephanotis floribunda Position in mostly indirect sunlight.

Thunbergia alata Some direct sunlight every day is essential for good display of its orange, yellow, or white flowers.

Bird's-nest ferns and fig plants

Plants for the hallway

The porch, entrance hallway, or corridor may be bright or shady but they share the common problem of being prone to drafts. Sudden changes in temperature as well as rapid changes in humidity can affect many plants.

Most plants grow best where the conditions change very little on a day-to-day basis. For this situation, you will need to look for tolerant flowering and foliage plants (to suit the available light levels) that will not mind the fluctuating temperatures and conditions.

When looking for a suitable site to place your plants in the entrance hall or corridor, make sure that they will not be in a position where they will be continually brushed up against by people walking past. Flowering plants can easily have their blooms knocked off, and the leaves of foliage plants can become battered and browned at the edges, which can eventually impede their growth. Place on a pedestal table or on a ledge, if there is one in the hallway.

PLANTS FOR THE HALLWAY

Argyranthemum frutescens Keep soil mix moist.

Campanula isophylla Deadhead to prolong flowering.

Cyclamen persicum Keep cool with moderate light.

Eustoma grandiflorum Enjoys indirect sunlight.

x *Fatshedera lizei* Increase humidity in warmer locations.

Hedera helix Tolerates a wide range of temperatures.

Impatiens spp. Enjoys average temperatures.

Narcissus cvs. Keep cool and away from direct sunlight.

Pelargonium spp. Tolerates direct or indirect sunlight.

Pericallis x *hybrida* Keep out of direct sunlight.

Primula Pruhonicensis hybrids Choose a lightly shaded location.

Rosa spp. Indirect sunlight, cool location.

Saxifraga stolonifera In higher temperatures, increase humidity.

Sparrmannia africana Place in indirect sunlight in a cool position.

Thunbergia alata Keep thoroughly moist in a cool room.

Tolmeia menziesii Tolerates most conditions, but not intense sunlight or shade.

Tradescantia spp. Needs some direct sunlight every day to maintain leaf color.

Daffodils (*Narcissus* cvs.) will tolerate the cooler, drafty conditions that tend to pertain in entrance hallways and porches.

Exacum affine

Plants for the bathroom

The atmosphere in the bathroom tends to vary widely from hot and steamy when it is in use to cool and drier when it is not. The steam means that the humidity level is higher than elsewhere in the house, but the plant needs to be able to withstand the fluctuating temperatures.

Ferns are a good choice for this environment, as long as the temperature does not drop too low, as are dramatic foliage plants and tolerant species such as the spider plant.

Bathrooms are ideal for these plants, and the environment will prevent foliage from turning brown at the edges—which happens if they are kept in positions without high humidity. Position in groups of the same plant or have a variety of different plants.

The cristate table fern (*Pteris cretica* 'Alexandrae') looks fabulous displayed in a bathroom.

PLANTS FOR THE BATHROOM

Achimenes spp. Keep out of direct sunlight.

Adiantum spp. Do not allow roots to be too wet or dry out.

Aeschynanthus speciosus Water well, even in a bathroom.

Anthurium scherzerianum If in doubt, mist regularly.

Asparagus densiflorus 'Sprengeri' Avoid direct sunlight because this may scorch the feathery green foliage.

Begonia spp. Remove any damaged or dying leaves as soon as they are spotted.

Brunfelsia pauciflora 'Macrantha' Position in direct sunlight.

Dracaena cvs. Keep compost moist from spring to autumn.

Exacum affine Pick off fading flowers to extend flowering.

Gardenia augusta Keep draft-free while buds are forming.

Impatiens New Guinea hybrids Place in a location that is not too warm.

Nephrolepis exaltata 'Bostoniensis' Keep constantly moist.

Peperomia spp. Keep only barely moist at all times.

Pteris cretica Position out of direct sunlight and keep moist.

Primula obconica

Plants for garden rooms

Greenhouses, garden rooms, terraces, and sunrooms offer a range of growing conditions, all different from those found inside the home. These rooms provide excellent places to sit and enjoy your plants, almost as if you were sitting in the garden.

The higher light levels in porches or sunrooms mean that plants will grow well. However, scorch may be a problem on susceptible plants unless shade can be provided from the most intense sun around midday. Drafts are more of a problem here than indoors, so choose plants that are tolerant of the conditions or that enjoy a period outdoors in summer. The more protected the situation, the greater the range of plants that can be grown. Make the best of the surroundings, and use specimen plants to make a serious impact.

A greenhouse provides the ideal environment for tender plants, such as this rhododendron, which needs to be brought inside to overwinter.

PLANTS FOR A PORCH OR SUNROOM

Allamanda cathartica Climber, suited to a warm greenhouse.

Argyranthemum cvs. Water generously, especially in summer.

Begonia spp. Ideal under glass, out of direct sunlight.

Bougainvillea glabra Needs high levels of warmth and light to flower well.

x *Citrofortunella* Ornamental orange, ideal for a greenhouse.

Citrus spp. Interesting genus, producing flowers and fruit.

Dracaena Foliage plants grown for their striking leaves.

Fatsia japonica Makes an impressive specimen plant.

Hibiscus 'Luna' Enjoys full sunlight and produces huge, showy flowers.

Mandevilla spp. Large, showy climber for indirect sunlight.

Nerium oleander Ideal for a bright, well-lit garden room.

Pentas lanceolata Prefers direct sunlight, but not too hot.

Plumbago auriculata This shrub has pretty, sky blue flowers

Primula obconica Group together for instant effect.

Rhododendron simsii Spectacular display of flowers.

Rosa spp. Great for the terrace garden, but bring in over winter.

Sollya heterophylla Perfect climber for any garden room.

Thunbergia alata Train up a tepee of canes.

Zantedeschia aethiopica Fairly hardy; perfect for a terrace.

Low-maintenance plants

There are times when, for one reason or another, you want the benefit of houseplants but have little time to take care of them. This is the time to look for those tolerant species that can cope with erratic watering and are capable of recovering if they are slightly neglected.

A grouping of peperomias

You can help a plant by not leaving it situated on a windowsill, where it could dry out quicker—a wilted plant is a sure sign to burglars that the house is empty anyway. Instead, place it on a saucer of wet pebbles, and group a few plants together so that they form a microclimate under their leaves and keep the humidity higher.

Low-maintenance plants still need attention, so whenever you can, spend time making sure that they are watered, fed, and in the correct size pot. If you are going away for a short period, carrying out these few tasks will help your plants survive until the next time they can be watered. If you are going to be away from the house frequently, make sure you select the right group of plants in the first place. Choose plants with thick, leathery leaves because they are adapted to conserving moisture. Plants with thin, delicate leaves will not recover well from water deprivation.

LOW-MAINTENANCE PLANTS

Chlorophytum comosum Makes a dramatic trailing plant if its container is placed on a pedestal.

Clivia miniata Keep almost dry during winter.

Desert cacti These cacti have a waxy outer covering and ridges on their stems, and their leaves have become spines or hairs.

x *Fatshedera lizei* Evergreen shrub, easy to cultivate.

Fatsia japonica Impressive specimen plant that grows rather quickly.

Monstera deliciosa Once established and trained up a support, this plant is fairly easy to look after and cultivate.

Nerium oleander Can be kept barely moist during winter.

Peperomia spp. All have fleshy, waxy leaves and can be kept barely moist at all times.

Philodendron bipinnatifidum Keep moist from spring to autumn, just enough to stop drying out in winter.

Pilea cadierei Very easy to grow if kept in partial shade and barely moist.

Sanseveria trifasciata. Extremely tolerant of neglect and able to survive in hardy environments.

Desert cacti such as *Opuntia microdasys* can withstand periods of drought in the home.

Trailing houseplants

Plants that have a naturally trailing or creeping habit make an interesting addition to any display. They have a multitude of uses, from brightening a plain wall in rooms inside the house, or outside walls under cover on a veranda, to trailing a lacy veil from a table.

Scindapsus pictus, S. 'Neon'

Planted along the edges of a large floor container, plants can blur and disguise the sharper edges as they grow over them. Dotted in among the other plants in the display, they can hide the growing medium and the bare stems of other plants.

Planted into a hanging basket or wall container, trailing plants will froth over the edge and cascade downward, forming a living fountain of color without taking up any floor space. This can be an effective way to add color where space is at a premium.

Alternatively, many trailing plants can be trained to grow up ornamental supports such as trellises, arbors, frames, or moss poles, adding to the garden display.

TRAILING HOUSEPLANTS

Chlorophytum comosum SPIDER PLANT. Makes a dramatic trailing plant when set in a hanging basket or on a pedestal.

Cissus antarctica KANGAROO VINE. Can be trained up a wall.

Dichondra 'Silver Falls' A true cascading habit.

Epipremnum aureum DEVIL'S IVY. Can be trained to climb up a moss pole or to cascade from a high planter or hanging basket.

Ficus pumila CREEPING FIG. Attractive groundcover or trailing plant.

Fittonia verschaffeltii MOSAIC PLANT. Ideal as a trailing plant in a terrarium.

Hedera spp. Can cover bare walls or weave around other plants or furniture.

Hoya lanceolata subsp. ***bella*** Miniature wax plant. Lovely scented flowers.

Lotus berthelotii PARROT'S BEAK. Brightly colored beaklike flowers.

Passiflora spp. PASSION FLOWER. Extremely attractive climber.

Philodendron bipinnatifidum Treelike shrub, climbing to 15 ft. (5 m) eventually.

Saxifraga stolonifera Cascading plantlets make for an attractive trailer.

Senecio macroglossus Slender, twining plant with succulent-looking leaves.

Thunbergia alata Quick-growing, twining plant with colorful flowers.

Tolmiea menziesii PICK-A-BACK PLANT. Attractive trailing plant in a hanging basket.

Tradescantia fluminensis WANDERING JEW. Tolerant, easy-to-grow trailer that hangs out of hanging baskets or sprawls profusely down shelves or bookcases.

A stunning hanging basket made up of foliage plants.

Fragrant flowering plants

There is nothing nicer than a pleasant scent to greet you as you enter a room. Natural air fresheners—like plants and flowers—are far less likely to induce a reaction than chemical ones, which can occasionally cause headaches in susceptible people.

Narcissus 'Tête-à-tête'

White flowers have the strongest scent because they have no color to attract pollinating insects. A little can go a long way, so try one plant before you introduce others. The fragrance from some, such as hyacinths, is seasonal, while others, such as *Citrus*, produce flowers intermittently throughout the year when they are growing in the right conditions.

A scented basket display of forced Dutch hyacinths provides a welcome splash of color and wonderful fragrance early in the year.

THE BEST OF FRAGRANT FLOWERING PLANTS

x ***Citrofortunella microcarpa*** White flowers and orange fruit.

Citrus Produces flowers and fruit intermittently throughout the year in the right conditions. Glossy, deep green foliage.

Dianthus 'Dynasty' CARNATIONS or PINKS. Multicolored varieties.

Freesia cvs. Bulbs with highly fragrant flowers, available in wide range of colors and providing a long-lasting display.

Gardenia augusta Bushy shrub with white blooms.

Hoya lanceolata subsp. ***bella*** Star-shaped flowers in clusters.

Hyacinthus orientalis Bright, multicolored waxy flowers.

Jasminum polyanthum Climber with tubular white flowers.

Lilium spp. & cvs. Bulbs with attractive, multicolored flowers.

Narcissus cvs. Genus is fragrant, but *N. papyraceus* (Paper-white narcissus) has highly scented white flowers.

Nerium oleander OLEANDER. Large shrub grown for its display of beautiful, funnel-shaped flowers.

Passiflora caerulea PASSION FLOWER. Stunning blooms.

Plumeria rubra Large, easy-to-grow shrub or small tree, producing attractive whitish flowers.

Stephanotis floribunda Train up against a wall beside a door or archway, where its fragrance can be appreciated.

Mixed herbs

Beneficial houseplants

Plants can improve the living environment in your home by absorbing carbon dioxide and toxins while giving off oxygen. They can also provide a way of introducing pleasant smells and fragrances into the home without the use of chemical or synthetic air fresheners.

The foliage of certain plants contains fragrant oils that are released as they are touched. Many of these plants, such as herbs, are useful in cooking and are easily grown indoors on a sunny windowsill. Others, such as *Pelargonium crispum* (lemon geranium), not only give off a delicate scent, they can also be used to add fragrance to your bath. Those that simply have scented foliage, such as *Lantana*, are best placed near a doorway so that their fragrance is released as you brush past.

One of the main allergens in the home is dust, so it is also essential to wipe plants with a damp cloth every week to prevent a layer of dust from building up. Avoid any plants that have hairy leaves that will trap dust and cannot be wiped clean as well as those that produce flowers with a heavy fragrance, such as lilies. Restrict the plants to living areas other than bedrooms and cover the medium with an inorganic mulch, such as fine gravel. An organic mulch might contain fungal spores.

AROMATIC FOLIAGE PLANTS

x *Citrofortunella* CALAMONDIN ORANGE. Produces fruit when still quite young. Glossy, deep green foliage with fragrant flowers.

Citrus spp. Given the correct warm conditions, these small trees can produce flowers and fruit all year long.

Lantana camara SHRUBBY VERBENA. Coarse-textured, dull, mid-green leaves, with multicolored blooms in summer.

Laurus nobilis BAY LAUREL. Cone-shaped shrub or small tree with aromatic, glossy dark green leaves.

Mentha spicata SPEARMINT or GARDEN MINT. Highly fragrant herb, useful in cooking.

Pelargonium crispum LEMON GERANIUM. Scented-leaf geranium grown for its aromatic foliage.

Thymus x *citriodorus* LEMON THYME. Shrubby herb, leaves give off a sharp lemon scent when crushed.

LOW-ALLERGY HOUSEPLANTS

Calathea makoyana PEACOCK PLANT or BRAIN PLANT. Dramatic, veined foliage.

Clivia miniata Glossy foliage.

Codiaeum variegatum CROTON or JOSEPH'S COAT. Glossy, heavily patterned leaves.

Dracaena cincta Striking, lance-shaped leaves.

x *Fatshedera lizei* Wide-spreading, attractive glossy leaves.

Ficus elastica RUBBER PLANT (*see* right).

Helianthus 'Ballad' DWARF SUNFLOWER. Bright center with bright golden yellow flowers, pollen-free.

Radermachera sinica Can tolerate the dry, centrally heated conditions of the modern house.

Sanseveria trifasciata Extremely tolerant of indoor conditions.

Houseplants that improve air quality

Many of the pieces of furniture and electrical equipment in our offices and homes release trace amounts of chemicals into the air, resulting in headaches and a feeling of lethargy. It has been proved that having plants around combats this effect. Plants absorb the toxins along with carbon dioxide and give off oxygen, making the environment cleaner and healthier. Large-leaved plants are the best choice. Keep them healthy and growing well so that they are constantly respiring and cleaning the air.

Foliage plants improve the atmosphere by absorbing toxins and dispensing oxygen.

HOUSEPLANTS THAT IMPROVE AIR QUALITY

Chamaedorea elegans PARLOR PALM. Graceful, arching leaves.

Codiaeum variegatum Leathery leaves, easy to clean.

Ctenanthe oppenheimiana Beautifully marked foliage.

Dieffenbachia seguine Grown for its decorative foliage.

Epipremnum aureum DEVIL'S IVY. Large, heart-shaped leaves.

x *Fatshedera lizei* Excellent attractive, spreading foliage.

Ficus elastica Glossy, leathery leaves.

Howea forsteriana KENTIA PALM. Enjoys a range of conditions.

Monstera deliciosa SWISS CHEESE PLANT. Distinctive leaves.

Musa acuminata Excellent for greenhouse border.

Philodendron bipinnatifidum Heart-shaped, wavy-edged lobes.

Pilea cadierei ALUMINUM PLANT. Oval leaves, toothed edges.

Radermachera sinica Fragrant yellow flowers on mature plants.

Solenostemon COLEUS. Semisucculent stems.

Gerberas

Selecting containers

Your new houseplant will, almost always, be in a plastic pot when you buy it. Plastic is lightweight, durable, and highly practical—but not necessarily attractive. Don't worry, there is a huge range of containers, cache pots, and other planters in which you can put your plant.

You can choose a style that reflects the surroundings where the plant will grow or something that is purely practical. The main factor to consider is drainage. It is critical that excess water be able to drain away from the root zone of the plant, or the plant will literally drown and the roots will die from a lack of oxygen. Allow for a saucer, or you will damage most surfaces, particularly polished wood. A cache pot will disguise a plastic pot and also serve to catch excess water, but make sure you drain off the surplus, or the plant will suffer.

Suiting the container to your interior

Containers are made of a multitude of different media and can be tailored to suit every situation.

Terra-cotta and earthenware pots, dishes, and cache pots are both attractive and practical. Most have a hole in the base and will need a saucer, but they are a natural color that blends well with the plants themselves. Moisture is lost through the sides of these pots as well as the base, so you may need to water the plants more frequently, and ideally, you should soak the pot for at least an hour before using it. They are available in plain or more decorative designs, with ornamental edges or relief patterns. Smaller terra-cotta pots are ideal for collections of similar plants, such as cacti or herbs, and suit a natural decor.

Ceramic and china containers are available in a vast range of shapes, colors, and designs. They can be chosen to team up with any design scheme, from the Victorian to the most modern. Particularly strong patterns or colors can distract attention away from the plant and overwhelm small-leaved specimens, so opt for more muted colors unless your plant is large or plain enough to withstand the competition. Ceramic pots with drainage holes will need a saucer; cache pots will not—they will need to be emptied of excess water. Unless the base is fully glazed, there may be a danger of moisture seeping through the base onto furniture.

Glass containers for plants grown in potting soil are unusual because the roots don't fare well in light, but they can be adapted. They are ideal for the modern or minimalist home because they do not intrude on the decor and can be extremely attractive in their own right. Hyacinth bulbs will grow in water in a glass container, but other plants will need to have the container lined with something to reduce the light transmission. You can use moss, gravel, or colored pebbles depending on the surroundings. There is no drainage in a glass container, so watering should be closely monitored to avoid waterlogging. Add a little charcoal to the mix as you plant to keep it fresh for longer.

Hyacinths can grow in special hyacinth glasses without soil mix.

Metal containers suit both the contemporary and the traditional home or work space. They can be left shiny or treated with paint to create the verdigris effect of aged copper. The container is unlikely to have drainage holes in the base, but they can be easily drilled into it. The only drawback of metal is that it heats up quickly in the sun, which can burn the roots of the plant, and does not retain any heat in the cold.

Wicker containers are made from the woven stems of willow, hazel, or grass. They are not watertight and are best used as a cover for the pot within, lined with black or brown plastic that will not show through the sides but will stop excess moisture from draining through the base. This natural material blends well with plants and decor of all kinds.

Wooden containers are so versatile that they can be chosen to suit many interiors, from the formal traditional to the rustic; from modern to Asian fusion. Wood is a natural material that is equally attractive left plain with the grain showing or painted to coordinate with its surroundings. It is not watertight and will need a plastic lining if you are planting directly into the container.

Bamboo containers are not common but are worth seeking out if your decor has been chosen with an Asian theme in mind. Like wood, this natural material will need lining with plastic to make it waterproof.

Plastic containers are the most commonly available and come in a huge range of shapes, sizes, and styles. They are lightweight, durable, easy to use, and do not need maintenance apart from a good scrub between plants. Plastic is used to mimic other materials, such as clay, providing imitations that are lighter and longer lasting.

Household items from old watering cans to teacups, kettles to casserole dishes, can be used to hold plants or their pots. This is particularly useful if you prefer a retro decor because you can suit the containers to whichever period you have selected.

Silver-painted pots surrounded by pebbles on a pewter tray make an attractive display for a group of mixed cacti and succulents.

Care of containers

Containers should last for many years, as long as they are well cared for and not damaged in any way. If you are using a container again, it needs to be cleaned thoroughly with hot soapy water to avoid spreading any disease from one plant to another.

Preparing and maintaining your containers

Terra-cotta is a porous material that can hold a lot of moisture. New pots need soaking in water for at least half an hour before use to prevent their drawing moisture from the soil and depriving the plant.

Metal pots should be lined with plastic to prevent their minerals from affecting the growing medium. Wooden containers can also be lined with plastic to stop wood rot from coming in close contact with the constantly damp soil mix. In each case, drainage holes need to be made in the base to prevent waterlogging.

Avoid damaging the roots

Planting and potting

In the wild, plant roots grow into new soil throughout the season in search of food and water. In a container, the roots still need to grow, but the restricted room for expansion means that unless more space is provided, the roots will circle around and around inside the pot.

Cramped conditions will result in a "pot-bound" plant, with slow growth and poor flowers. Most plants need moving into a new, slightly larger pot with fresh soil mix once a year, normally in the spring as the new growth for the season starts.

The term "planting" generally refers to placing young plants, bulbs, corms, or tubers into permanent positions in containers of soil mix. Check that the new container has drainage holes in the base to prevent waterlogging and that it is at least 2 in. (5 cm) larger than the old one.

This mature *Crassula ovata* needs the top
inch of soil mix replaced regularly.

REPOTTING PLANTS

When to repot:

- when the root-ball is congested (roots showing through the base of the pot or on the surface of the soil mix).
- if the plant is drying out more quickly than usual on a regular basis (too many roots in the pot and too little soil mix).
- if the rate of growth has slowed down noticeably.
- if the top growth has become lopsided (this can be corrected by centering the plant in a larger pot).
- if the plant seems loose or poorly anchored.
- if the plant has become overcrowded in the pot due to offsets that can be separated and propagated in their own right.
- if the growing medium is to be changed (for instance, to hydroculture).
- if an attack of pests or disease is damaging the roots (they can be washed in water or fungicide and replanted into fresh soil mix).

Lay a piece of newspaper across the base to stop the mix from falling through the holes. Stand the plant inside to gauge the level, adding more soil mix underneath if necessary; then fill up around the sides, firming gently with your fingertips. Fill the pot to 1 in. (2.5 cm) below the rim, then water it to settle the soil mix and add more if any holes appear.

Repotting

This is the term used when the plant is put back into the same container with fresh soil mix, rather than being moved to a new one. If the plant is moved into an entirely new container—normally because it has outgrown its original pot—this is known as "transplanting."

Transplanting

Young, actively growing plants need to be moved on a regular basis to make sure that they have enough room to grow without suffering a check because their roots are cramped. How often this needs to be done will depend on the plant itself. Quick-growing specimens in ideal conditions need to be transplanted more often than slower growing ones.

1 *Select a pot that is comfortably larger than the one currently occupied by the plant, so it has plenty of extra room.*

2 *Once you are satisfied that the new pot will give the plant room to grow, place the plant in the pot.*

3 *Fill around the sides of the root-ball with fresh soil mix and water the plant thoroughly to give it a good new start.*

Removing a plant from a small pot

Whenever a plant is removed from a container, it is important to avoid causing damage to the roots because open wounds are potential sites for attack by disease. To make the operation smoother, thoroughly water the plant at least an hour before attempting to remove the pot. This will hold the soil mix together and will allow the root-ball to be easily slipped from the old pot.

1 *Place one hand over the soil surface, straddling the stem. Tap the edge on a solid item to loosen the plant in the pot.*

2 *Ease the plant gently from the pot, taking care not to damage the root-ball as you jiggle it free.*

3 *Transfer the plant to the new pot, add more compost and water thoroughly to settle the plant in its new pot.*

Watering a bromeliad rosette

Routine care

Plants can tolerate deficiencies in light and nutrients for a while, but if you deprive a plant of water, it will die. How long this takes depends on the plant. A succulent, which stores moisture within its tissue, will last much longer than a young seedling, which has no reserves to draw upon.

The water taken up by a plant is used to transport chemicals around within the cells, moving nutrients up from the roots, and sugars and starches down from the leaves. It keeps the plant turgid (firm to the touch and able to support its own weight), the cells full, and allows the chemical reactions that keep the plant alive (such as photosynthesis) to happen.

Watering

Without adequate water, the plant's health suffers and its cells start to deflate, resulting in a flaccid plant as the cell walls lose contact with the surrounding cells. Nutrients and sugars can no longer pass through the plant and the structure begins to collapse as moisture is still constantly lost (transpiration) from pores on the leaf surfaces (stomata) due to internal pressure. Getting the watering just right is often a matter of trial and error because every plant is different and each will change throughout its life and at different times of the year.

When to water depends on the requirements of the individual plant. There are various indicators available to help the beginner, but there is no real substitute for practice and observation. By the time the plant wilts, it may be too late to save it, so check it regularly. Lift the pot up (the lighter the pot, the drier it is); touch the soil mix to feel how dry it is; if the plant is in a clay pot, look at the outside, because the wetter it is, the darker the pot will be.

Watering tips

Plants like rosette-forming bromeliads need watering into their central cups as well as the pots because they absorb moisture through their leaves.

Plants with hairy leaves need watering from below, because any water on the surface of the leaves is trapped in place by the hairs and will cause scorching as it magnifies the light.

A water indicator changes color as the soil mix dries out, indicating that more water is required.

Reviving a wilted plant

Plunge it in a bucket of water (containing a small drop of dishwashing liquid in order to speed up penetration of the compost, particularly if it is peat-based) and hold it there until bubbles stop rising. Leave the plant to drain.

Draining an over-watered plant

Overwatering does not compensate for under-watering and causes additional problems. Tip the pot on an angle against the rim of a saucer until the excess water stops running out. Do not apply more water for several days.

How much water to apply

To keep a plant thoroughly moist, apply enough water to keep the soil mix completely moist all of the time, though never actually wet. Even the surface should not be allowed to dry out. Check your plants thoroughly every day.

To keep a plant moist, apply enough water each time to moisten the compost completely, but allow the top ½–1 in. (1–2 cm) to dry out before re-watering. Check every 2–3 days.

To keep it slightly dry, apply enough water each time to moisten the compost completely, but allow the top half of the compost to dry out before re-watering. Check once a week.

The plant may only need to be kept sufficiently moist to prevent the soil mix from drying out through the resting period when very little moisture is needed, because cell-operations are at a bare minimum. It should be checked once a week and given only enough water to keep the compost barely moist. However, once growth starts again in spring, the plant will immediately need an increased amount of water, and within two weeks, it will be back to its normal requirement.

Final thoughts

Everyone gets plant care wrong sometimes, and unless it is taken to extremes, it is rarely fatal. Recognizing and dealing with a problem quickly is the key to a good recovery.

QUICK-REFERENCE WATERING GUIDE

How much water to apply depends on various factors.

Plants need more when they:

- are growing quickly (when they are young and in spring as they come out of the resting period)
- are coming up to, or are in, flower
- have filled their current pot and are in need of repotting
- are in a hot or dry atmosphere
- are in clay pots (moisture is lost through the sides as well as at the surface)
- are moisture-lovers
- are growing in a peat-based soil, or peat-substitute because these dry out quickly

Plants need less when they:

- are resting, usually, although not necessarily, during the winter months
- store moisture within their leaves and/or stems
- have a waxy covering on their leaves that reduces moisture loss
- are growing in cool or humid conditions
- have been recently repotted
- are in plastic pots
- are growing in a loam-based soil mix because this holds moisture longer
- are in a self-contained environment, such as a terrarium

Feeding

In the wild, plants draw the nutrients and minerals they need from the soil by extending their roots. In containers, both the room for root expansion and the amount of medium are drastically reduced, so it is important to replace the nutrients on a regular basis to maintain healthy growth.

Fertilizers

The two main types of fertilizer available for plants are classed as organic or inorganic.

Organic fertilizers are made from a plant or animal base and tend to be absorbed slowly by the plant, which means they are longer lasting.

Inorganic fertilizers are mineral-based and are generally faster acting but tend to be used up more quickly.

All plants require three main chemical elements for healthy growth:

nitrogen (N) for shoots and leaves
phosphorus (P) for roots
potassium (K) for fruits and flowers

The amount of each of these in relation to the others in a compost or fertilizer is shown on the pack as the N:P:K ratio, and for a balanced general fertilizer, the number given will be the same for each element, such as 7:7:7.

Plants have different requirements for these elements, as well as a number of trace elements including iron, copper, zinc, magnesium, and manganese. For instance, foliage plants have a lower requirement for potassium than plants grown for flowers, but they have a higher need for nitrogen. However, a flowering plant will need a balance of all three main elements, and change to an emphasis on potassium as the buds develop.

Types of fertilizers

Plant fertilizers contain the three main nutrients, plus a full range of trace elements, and are available in a variety of forms, as either quick-release or slow-release, depending on how quickly they dissolve in water.

Liquid feeds (including soluble powder, granules, and crystals) have an immediate effect because they are easily absorbed and the plant usually responds within a week.

Foliar fertilizers are applied to plants that do not easily take nutrients through the roots, such as Bromeliads, are absorbed directly by the leaves, and can act as a rapid pick-me-up for an ailing plant.

Pellets, pins, and pills are placed in the soil mix in a solid form and are slower to become available to the plant. Don't push them too close to the roots, or scorching may occur.

High-potash (potassium) fertilizer spikes are designed to release nutrients gradually when the plant is watered.

EFFECTS OF OVERFERTILIZING
• the leaves show signs of wilting and/or malformations
• there are brown spots and/or scorched edges to the leaves
• a white encrustation develops on the surface of the soil mix
• the growth is long and drawn in winter, stunted in summer

EFFECTS OF UNDER-FERTILIZING
• the plant has slow, sickly looking growth
• there is little resistance to disease or pest attack
• the flowers are poorly colored and small or missing entirely
• leaves are small, dull, pale colored, and often shed early

When to fertilize

Fresh soil mix contains nutrients that will be adequate for the plant initially, but how long they last depends on the type of plant, its growth rate, and whether the soil mix is loam-based or loamless. Loam (sterilized natural soil) contains nutrients and holds additional ones better than peat, which tends to release them as water passes through.

Start fertilizing plants after 6–8 weeks in a loamless compost and 10–12 weeks in a loam-based one, then feed regularly during the active growing and flowering season.

Plants bought from the garden center will not have been fed for two weeks prior to leaving the nursery (so a build-up of fertilizer caused by erratic watering will not damage the roots) and will need fertilizing immediately.

Most plants have a resting period during the winter months, when they do not need fertilizing, with the exception of plants that flower at Christmas and will need fertilizing then rather than during the spring or summer.

How to fertilize

Liquid formulations come as a concentrate, as dry granules, or powder to be diluted with, or dissolved in, water, and applied using a watering can, or in the case of a liquid foliar feed, a mist sprayer.

Dry formulations are added to the soil mix when the plant is potted, or as a topdressing on the surface of an older plant.

Pins and spikes are pushed into the soil mix with the end of a pencil—take care not to place them too close to the roots, because localized burning can occur as a result of the high concentration of fertilizer. They cannot be "switched off" as the plant goes into its winter resting period, and may cause weak, elongated growth.

The growing medium

Plants have certain requirements of the medium in which they are growing, whether it is indoors or out. They need a firm anchorage for their roots, the correct pH level, and a readily accessible supply of air, water, and nutrients in an environment free from pests and diseases.

In the case of a medium for indoor use, this means that the soil mix has to be:
• sterile; pH neutral (unless it is specifically designed for acid-loving plants);
• firm enough to support the plant and keep it upright, but still be lightweight and hold air;
• able to supply the roots with the water and nutrients they need to grow, without letting the plant become water-logged.

There are two main choices of soil mix: loam-based (which contain soil) and loamless (which are based on peat or a peat-substitute).

The loam-based composts hold nutrients and moisture better than loamless composts, and are more stable. But they are heavier, and more suitable for older plants, which are likely to be in their pots for some time, or for floor-based specimens that need the extra weight to prevent them from being knocked over. Loamless composts are light, clean, and easy to handle, but they are inclined to dry out (and difficult to re-wet), and nutrients are washed through them fairly quickly.

Soil mix and drainage

There are a variety of other substances which can be added to the basic ingredients, including Perlite, vermiculite, sand, and grit, all of which to allow more air into the compost and speed up the drainage.

Potting and repotting

Every plant benefits from fresh soil mix annually, but if it is in the largest container you can accommodate, there is no reason to change it. Likewise, as a plant ages and its rate of growth slows down, it may only be necessary to move it into a larger pot in alternate years rather than every year. You can refresh the soil mix in the same container by changing some or all of the compost instead. Remove the root-ball from the pot and very gently wash some of the old compost away from the roots without damaging them in any way. Return it to the same container and fill around the roots with a new soil mix that contains a slow-release fertilizer that will last until it needs repotting again.

The newly bought plant

When a plant is first purchased, the chances are that it is already becoming pot-bound, because most plants, especially foliage ones, are sold in the smallest possible pot in order to make the plant look larger (and therefore, a better value).

The easiest way to tell if this is the case is to examine the base of the pot for protruding roots—the more there are, the more pot-bound the plant is likely to be. It will need transplanting into a larger pot immediately to keep it actively growing. Tease out a few of the main roots as it is planted to help the plant adjust to its new pot and start to grow. Trim off a few of the main roots at this stage to slow the growth of the plant down if it is likely to grow too quickly for its surroundings.

Handling a difficult plant

1 *The following method is a good way to handle prickly plants such as cacti, as well as cactus plants with irritating sap. Cactus spines in the skin can cause discomfort for weeks and the easiest way to avoid this is by not touching the plant directly at all. Wrap a piece of folded newspaper or cloth around the plant and use it to cover the compost as the pot is inverted and knocked on a table edge to loosen the root-ball.*

2 *Continue to leave the newspaper or cloth wrapped around the plant throughout the procedure as it is transferred to its new container, and then use it to hold the plant in place as the compost is filled in and firmed around the sides. Discard the cloth only once the whole operation is complete and the plant is safely in its new pot. Other awkward-to-handle plants can also be treated this way.*

Problems with mature plants

As plants age and their root systems expand to fill their pots, the compost is literally squeezed out of the base, leaving progressively less to provide water and nutrients. This may even be the case when a plant is first purchased, where the root-ball is so congested that roots are protruding through the base of the pot.

Removing the pot in the conventional way would damage the roots as they are dragged back through the holes in the base, so the pot has to be cut away using heavy scissors, or broken off in the case of terra-cotta. The long roots will soon reestablish once the plant has more room to grow.

With established plants, the rate of growth of the roots is directly related to the rate of top growth. Trimming back the main roots will control the top growth when the plant has reached the desired size.

Mature roots protruding through the pot.

Scrape away the top, old layer of soil mix.

Top-dressing a mature plant

Removing a plant from its pot, however briefly, can cause it stress, and mature plants find it more difficult to cope with than young ones.

As an alternative to regularly repotting a mature plant, which causes disturbance, it can be top-dressed instead. Outdoors, this would mean applying a fertilizer around the base of a plant. But indoors it includes adding new soil mix in the upper part of the pot. The plant can then stay in place for up to two years before it needs repotting. The old soil mix is gently scraped away, discarded, and replaced by the same amount of fresh soil to mix—usually containing a slow-release fertilizer.

Decorative mulches

Soil mix in a container is not the most attractive material. A decorative mulch will help disguise it by providing a much more appealing covering around the plant. However, it will also serve a useful purpose by reducing the moisture that is constantly lost from the compost by evaporation and ensuring that more mositure is available to the plant.

Gravel, pebbles, and chipped granite all provide a natural mulch in neutral or pale colors that will not detract from the plant. However, they are all relatively heavy and are best suited to a more permanent planting. Fine aquarium gravel is ideal for use around desert cacti.

Cocoa shell and bark are much lighter in weight, and the shell gives off a wonderful scent of chocolate when first added to the pot.

Decorative mulches add interest to displays.

Pruning and preening

Pruning can be practiced for several reasons. Its main purpose is to remove the three *d's*: dead, damaged or diseased stems and any crossing or rubbing stems. It controls vigor, and can be used to promote flowering or fruit production.

Rejuvenating a bougainvillea

Pruning can be done at any time as the need arises, although the benefit is greatest in spring, when the new growth will respond quickly. As you work, be aware of the plant's sap, which may irritate the skin.

Many indoor plants are too small, soft, or sappy to need much in the way of pruning, apart from dead-heading as the flowers fade to encourage the formation of more buds and prevent the old ones from rotting. Woody plants will need more attention to keep the growth healthy and going in the right direction.

Plants with a bushy habit will need the growing points taken off the main shoots regularly to encourage the development of side branches, which should be tipped to produce a rounded shape. If the plant has variegated foliage, any shoots that revert to plain green need to be removed, because the increased chlorophyll in these leaves makes this growth stronger, and it will take over and dominate if left in place.

Pinching, tipping, and bushing

Supplies of natural growth-regulating hormones within a plant are found in the highest concentrations in the growing points of shoots, where they act to suppress competition from the other buds down the stems. If these tips are removed, the hormones in the other buds are triggered into action, producing a side shoot from almost every leaf axil. This is known as "bushing." In nature, this is intended to provide another leading shoot to assume dominance, but pinching can be used on domestic plants to encourage dense, bushy growth. Manipulating growth in

this way is known as "pinching" on a younger plant—it is normally done using the finger and thumb and can also be used to encourage climbing plants to produce multiple stems. It is called "tipping" on an older plant, when secateurs are often used for trimming.

Pruning cuts

The positioning of the cut is critical—too close to the bud and it will die, too far away and the dying stub of stem is a target for disease.

Alternate buds—*The cut should slant upwards to just above an outward-facing bud, without being too close or touching it.*

Opposite buds—*the cut should be made straight across the stem above the buds, taking care not to harm them.*

Remedial pruning

1 *Remedial pruning maintains the health of a plant and it is generally carried out on older plants or those that have suffered damage. It includes cutting out dead and diseased parts of the plant and any stems that might have been damaged.*

2 *Woody plants often benefit from a remedial trim to thin out overcrowded stems or to remove any stems that are crossing and might rub together, opening up a wound in the stems where disease could enter the plant.*

3 *A plain green stem on a variegated plant will need to be removed as soon as it is noticed. Because there is no chlorophyll in the yellow or white parts of the variegated leaves and their growth is correspondingly slower, an all-green shoot will soon take over and dominate.*

4 *Remedial pruning can be done any time it is required, but flowers will be lost if it is happens as the buds are developing. As a rule, it is best to wait until the plant has finished flowering before pruning.*

Rejuvenating plants

Severe pruning to rejuvenate a plant is a fairly extreme technique because plants will respond only if they have the ability to regrow from the base. For those that do, it allows them to remain in the home rather than being discarded. It is useful if the plant has been purchased in flower but looks straggly as the flowers die off. Cutting the old stems off close to the base will provide strong new replacement stems, which can be trained as they grow. Flowering may be sacrificed for a year, but the result will be a much more attractive plant.

This plant's stems have been cut right down.

Deadheading

Dying flowers on a plant not only look unsightly, but they are liable to rot as they fall and are a prime target for attack by gray mold (botrytis). This can quickly spread to the rest of the plant if there are any damaged areas where it can enter. The whole flower head should be removed, including any developing seeds, because unless the seed is going to be collected and used, its production wastes the plant's energy. With many plants, removing the flowers as they fade encourages the production of more buds, because their natural instinct is to produce seed. This extends the flowering season and increases the interest of the plant.

Removing the flower head.

Training

Many of the plants grown indoors are rampant climbers, trailers, and scramblers, which hold on to their supports by means of aerial roots, twining tendrils, or twisting stems. These plants need training against a trellis or frame to keep their growth—which is often inclined to be straggly if left to itself—under control. Plants such as *Thunbergia*, *Hoya*, and *Ficus pumila* naturally trail, but they can be grown against frames to display their flowers or foliage to full advantage. The support should suit the plant: A large plant, such as *Monstera*, needs a strong moss pole or sturdy frame; a delicate plant, such as *Passiflora*, needs a much finer support, so that one does not outweigh the other.

Plants for training

Young plants can be trained on smaller frames, but the larger ones will need to progress to a more substantial support as they grow.

Training on wall/large frame:

• *Bougainvillea, Cissus, Hedera, Jasminum, Passiflora*
• *Thunbergia*

Training on a moss pole:

• x *Fatshedera lizei, Ficus pumila, Monstera, Philodendron*

Training on a small frame:

• *Ficus pumila, Hoya, Pelargonium*

Stakes and supports

Stakes and supports should to enhance the appearance of the plant without being obvious. Indoors, plants tend to be grown individually, rather than massed together as they might in the garden. This means that they cannot rely on each other for support and must have it provided.

Using a frame to support the plant not only allows it to be trained to grow in a certain direction—it takes the strain off the stems, reduces stress, and allows it to concentrate its energies on growing and flowering. It holds the plant firmly in place, reducing the chance of it falling over, and can be used to increase the airflow between the stems, lowering the chance of an attack by fungal disease.

Moss pole

Many plants climb by means of aerial roots that anchor themselves into moist crevices in the surrounding rocks and trees. Without this moisture, the roots will shrivel and die and the support will be lost. Indoors, this environment can be recreated using moist sphagnum moss either wired around a cane or packed inside a wire tube. The moss forms a continuous column that can draw moisture up from the potting soil.

1 Wrap the wire into a tube and bend the ends over to hold it closed.

2 Fill with moist sphagnum moss, add soil mix to the pot, and position inside the pot.

3 Hold the stems in place with hoops of plastic-covered wire pressed into the moss.

4 Space the plants evenly around the pole, fill in with soil mix, and mist thoroughly.

Types of support

The type of support used should suit the plant and the situation. Supports are available in a wide variety of materials, including bamboo, plastic, metal, rattan, and wood, or as raffia- or moss-filled poles. In an ornamental situation, the support can be an ornate design, or it can be painted to complement the surroundings. In a temporary or purely functional situation, plain bamboo canes may be all that are required.

A support should be firmly anchored so there is no possibility of the plant pulling it down as it grows and its weight increases. This means that wall supports need to be fixed securely to the wall with several heavy-duty screws or nails, and pot-held frames need to be pushed well down into the potting soil to hold them safely. Be sure to take the overall height of a pot into consideration, because the growing plant could make it top-heavy.

Ties

Plant stems can be tied in place using string, twist ties, wire rings, or raffia. They should be fixed tightly enough to hold them in place, but not so constricting that they bite into the tissue. Stems can also be held in place against a wall by using nails with plastic hoops attached (used for holding cabling in place) and garden twine as a tie.

Vacation care

During a short vacation, plants can survive without special treatment, as long as they are thoroughly watered beforehand and moved to a cool position. However, for a longer period, it will be necessary to make contingency plans.

There are a number of ways in which plants can be watered even during a holiday period when no one is there to care for them.

Wicks and capillary matting both work by allowing plants to suck up as much water as they need from a reservoir. This will not work if the matting dries out and the capillary column is broken, because it cannot be re-established without help. A piece of plastic film may have to be laid over the wick to keep it moist. Alternatively, placing newspaper around the plant helps to retain moisture.

Wicks—*Each presoaked wick is placed into a pot by pushing it in through the base or by removing the plant from the pot, placing the wick at the side, and replacing the plant. The more contact the wick has with the soil mix, the better. The free end of the wick is then placed in a container of water where it can soak.*

Presoaked capillary matting—*This can cope with a greater number of plants and is placed partially into a plugged sink containing 4–6 in. (10–15 cm) of water and partially on the draining board. The pots are then placed directly onto the matting.*

Moist pebbles—*A tray of moist pebbles is a less-controlled method of keeping plants moist by grouping them together in the tray. The roots can stay moist as long as the water level in the tray does not drop too far. But it is important that the level is not too high initially, or the roots may become too wet and rot.*

Water-retaining gel—*These crystals absorb many times their own weight of water, hold it, and release it back to the plants on demand. They then absorb more water when it becomes available, keeping the moisture level in the compost much more even and compensating for erratic water application.*

Vine weevils

Pests and diseases

Ours is not an ideal world and not everything that comes into contact with our plants is beneficial. Even the best-cared-for plant can fall victim to a random attack by a pest or disease, or suffer due to a sudden physiological condition.

The key to bringing a plant through a problem with a minimum amount of damage is to identify and deal with it quickly. Keeping the plant in a healthy, well-fed condition also helps, because a plant under stress, for whatever reason, is a plant vulnerable to attack and lacking the resources to fight it off.

Not every condition will mean reaching for the chemical spray, although it may be the only answer to a really persistent problem. Often, inverting a plant into a bowl or bucket of soapy water may be enough to cure a minor attack of greenfly, for example. If chemicals are needed, they should be used strictly in accordance with the manufacturer's instructions on the package, and sensible precautions must be taken if they are recommended, such as wearing gloves or a face mask. Children and pets should be kept out of the way while the chemical is applied.

Whenever a plant begins to look "out of sorts," or just not as good as usual, it is worth running through a quick mental checklist to establish a cause:

• when was it last watered or fed?
• has the humidity level changed?
• could it have been chilled or overheated?
• is there a visible pest?
• is there sign of disease?
• is there serious distortion on the plant?

Correct identification of the problem is crucial to the treatment, but it can be hampered by the fact that identical symptoms may have differing causes.

After identifying the problem, the next step is to deal with it. This is easier for some conditions than others and it may be preferable to put the plant into isolation while it is being treated, before it becomes a hazard to its neighbors. For instance, a fungus such as gray mold will attack any plant if it has damaged tissue where the spores can find a point of entry. If the plant is treated with a chemical, either as a spray or a drench, it is safer to apply it outdoors on a calm day.

Diseases and physiological disorders are much more difficult to identify than pests, where you can usually see a definite culprit. Fungi and bacteria are microscopic organisms that invade unnoticed. Unless the symptoms of attack are seen and dealt with promptly, they can be fatal, not only to the initial host but to other nearby plants as well, as the organism spreads. Viruses can be passed on in cuttings from one generation to the next, and while the resulting leaf markings can be attractive (as in several varieties of camellia), they can sometimes cause serious distortion.

Physiological problems arise most often when the care instructions for a particular plant have not been followed closely enough. It is important to the health of the plant to try to give it the conditions it needs to live in, regular food, sufficient water, and plenty of room for the roots to expand.

Pests

SYMPTOMS	CONDITION	PREVENTION	CONTROLS
Plant wilts for no apparent reason.	Ant attack	Put containers on "pot feet" to lift them off the floor. Keep plants watered; ants prefer dry conditions.	Use peppermint oil to deter insects or ant traps to ensure chemical is taken down into the nest to kill all the young.
Distorted shoot tips and new leaves. Sticky coating on leaves, sometimes with black, sooty mold.	Aphid attack	Remove and burn badly infected plants.	Invert smaller plants and submerge foliage in cool, soapy water. Spray larger plants with aphid control.
	Blackfly attack See Aphid		
Holes eaten in leaves, flowers, and seed pods. Plant may be defoliated. Butterfly and moth larvae with smooth or hairy tubular bodies are found.	Caterpillar attack	Check plants when they are brought inside after being outdoors in summer.	Remove small amounts by hand. For larger infestations, use systemic insecticide.
Leaves and stems of cyclamen become brittle and distorted; flowers lose their color and wither. Minute insects that resemble dust.	Cyclamen mite	Only buy healthy-looking plants with clean, brown corms.	Destroy affected plants.
Small, circular notches or holes in leaves and flowers.	Earwig attack	Check plants when they are brought inside after being outdoors in summer.	Remove small numbers by hand. For larger infestations, use systemic insecticide.
Young plants and seedlings collapse.	Fungus gnat	Always use fresh, sterile soil mix.	For heavy infestations, use a systemic insecticide drench on the soil mix.
Pale green or white wiggly lines on leaves.	Leaf miner	Check plants when they are brought inside after being outdoors in summer.	Remove individual leaves by hand. For larger infestations, use systemic insecticide.
Patches of black sooty mold growing on sticky honeydew. Small fluffy white blobs on stems or leaves.	Mealy bug	Check plants as they are brought inside after being outdoors in summer.	Remove small amounts by hand. For larger infestations, use systemic insecticide.
Yellow, stunted growth, curled and mottled leaves covered with fine webbing as infestation progresses.	Red spider mite	Minute yellow-green, red, or pink mites that cluster on shoot tips. Check plants regularly for discolored leaves.	Spray with systemic insecticide as soon as symptoms are spotted and isolate plant to prevent spread.
Small brown, blisterlike bumps on stems and lower leaf surfaces. Sticky coating on leaves, sometimes with black, sooty mold.	Scale insect	Check plants when they are brought inside after being outdoors in summer.	Remove small numbers by hand. For larger infestations, use systemic insecticide.
Silvery mottling on leaf surfaces and white spots on flowers.	Thrips	Check plants as they are brought inside after being outdoors in summer.	Use systemic insecticide.
Notches eaten into the edges of leaves. Plant collapses and close examination reveals that the roots have been eaten.	Vine weevil	Check plants as they are brought inside after being outdoors in summer. Do not stack pots (it gives them somewhere to live).	Remove small amounts of adults by hand. For larger infestations, use systemic insecticide.
Plant looks discolored and unhealthy. Clouds of tiny white flies fly up if plant is disturbed. Honeydew (and black, sooty mold) may also be evident.	Whitefly	Adults are small winged insects, nymphs look like flat, white, oval scales. Check underneath leaves regularly and thoroughly.	Use systemic insecticide.

Diseases

SYMPTOMS	CONDITION	PREVENTION	CONTROLS
Geranium and Pelargonium cuttings turn black at the base and die.	Black leg	Soil- or waterborne fungus, often carried on dirty tools. Keep working area and tools clean as you take cuttings of these plants.	Discard affected cuttings.
Seedlings wilt and die. Fungus spreads rapidly in the warm, humid conditions needed by seedlings.	Damping off	Always use clean seed trays or pots and sterile soil mix. Uncover the seedlings as soon as they are standing upright to allow air circulation.	Isolate affected tray/pot in a cooler, drier area. Some seedlings may survive.
Fuzzy gray covering affecting any aboveground part of the plant.	Gray mold	Botrytis fungus usually enters via a wound. Maintain good air circulation at all times. Clear away fallen leaves and flowers.	Prune any affected parts immediately.
White powdery covering on leaves and flowers. Distorted shoots and premature leaf fall.	Mildew	A parasitic fungus that invades soft plant tissue. Water regularly because stressed plants are more susceptible to attack.	Prune affected shoots. Use a general fungicide as a drench on the soil mix in case any spores remain.
Stems look wet and slimy, plant collapses.	Rot	Rot thrives in wet or very damp conditions, such as overwatering. Make sure plants do not sit in water for long periods.	Parts of the plant may be salvageable for cuttings, but otherwise discard.
Yellow blotches on leaf surfaces with bright orange or red-brown patches of spores on the undersides.	Rust	Fungus that attacks many indoor plants, especially Pelargoniums. Spreads rapidly. Space plants wide apart for good air circulation.	Remove affected leaves immediately. Use a copper-based fungicide for a severe infection or discard plants.
Black patches of mold on leaves, particularly lower ones.	Sooty mold	This fungus lives on the honeydew secreted by insectlike aphids. It looks unsightly and interferes with photosynthesis. Identify and treat pests quickly.	Wipe away mold with a soft cloth and cool, soapy water.
Leaves and shoots are small, distorted or grouped in unusual rosettes. Yellow distorted patterns on leaves.	Virus	Microscopic infection often carried by sapsucking insects and passed from plant to plant. Treat pests as soon as you see them.	Destroy affected plants. Do not propagate from them.

Care problems

SYMPTOMS	CONDITION	PREVENTION	CONTROLS
Slow, hard growth, sometimes with brown edges on the leaves.	Drafts	Sudden cold air lowers the temperature and humidity around the plant. Keep plants away from doors and frequently opened windows.	Move to a position with a constant temperature and mist to restore humidity.
Poor growth and flowering. Shedding of flower buds.	Erratic watering	Plants need a constant supply of water to survive. Interruptions will result in disrupted growth. Research the needs of the particular plant.	Establish a regular watering routine.

Care problems

SYMPTOMS	CONDITION	PREVENTION	CONTROLS
	Fluctuating temperatures See drafts		
Leaves become dry or develop brown edges. Plant falls victim to fungal attack.	Incorrect humidity	The amount of moisture in the air affects how much water is lost by the plant. Too little and leaves dry out, too much and fungal spores will thrive. Research the plant's needs.	Move the plant to a suitable position and mist regularly, if necessary.
White, powdery deposits on the leaves after watering.	Limescale	If water is high in calcium, a deposit is left on leaves if plant is watered from above. Always water into a saucer under the pot so water is taken up directly into the root zone.	Wipe away the deposit using a soft cloth and cool, soapy water.
Pale, soft, elongated growth. The plant is unable to support its own weight.	Low light	Plants need adequate light levels to photosynthesize their food and will grow in search of it. Research the needs of the particular plant.	Move the plant into a position with more suitable levels of light. Some pruning may be necessary to remove very extended shoots.
Growth may be stunted, yellow, purple, distorted, or mottled, depending on which mineral is missing. Poor flower formation.	Nutrient deficiency	Plants need a full range of minerals and trace elements to grow and flower properly. Research the needs of the particular plant.	Use a balanced fertilizer to restore the nutrients.
Plenty of lush green growth but no flowers.	Overfeeding	The usual culprit is excess nitrogen, which is ideal for foliage plants but reduces flowering. Research the needs of the particular plant.	Do not feed at all for six weeks. Then begin feeding again according to the plant's needs.
A variegated plant produces a completely green shoot.	Reversion	This is the plant reverting to its original form. The green shoot will be stronger, because it will contain more chlorophyll. If left, the variegation will be lost. Be vigilant.	Prune the green shoot out completely.
Brown dead spots or patches on leaves. Hot sun shining on leaves causes overheating and damage to cells. If droplets of water are left on the leaves, the effect is magnified.	Scorch	Keep plants with soft, sappy leaves out of direct sunlight. Very few plants can tolerate the intense sun at midday in summer.	Remove affected leaves if they are unsightly.
Plant wilts. Stem may be slimy. Soil mix smells stale.	Too much water	If there is too much water in the soil mix, there is no room for air. Without air, roots cannot breathe and the plant will literally drown. Research the needs of the particular plant.	Tip the pot at an angle to let the water drain out. Do not water again for 2-3 days.
Plant wilts. Leaves look pale and floppy. Pot is light in weight.	Too little water	Without adequate water, roots shrink and lose contact with the soil mix, cells shrink and nutrients are no longer moved around inside the plant. Research the plant's needs.	Submerge the root-ball in water until bubbles stop rising to the surface.
Growth is slow and hard, flowers do not form, stems may have a purple tint.	Underfeeding	Plants need a full range of minerals and trace elements to grow and flower properly. Research the needs of the particular plant.	Begin a regular routine for feeding according to the needs of the plant.
Growth slows down or stops during the winter months.	Winter dormancy	Most plants need a period of rest during the year between growing seasons. It coincides with low light levels and low temperatures. Research the plant's needs.	Water sparingly to avoid overwatering. Watch for growth restarting, then increase watering back to normal levels.

Removing an offset

Making more plants

There are many reasons for considering propagation in one of its many forms: If a plant has outgrown its allotted space; if it is looking old and fatigued; if someone has asked for a cutting; or perhaps simply for the challenge and satisfaction of producing a thriving new plant.

Two ways to produce one new plant from another are by cuttings (vegetative propagation) or seed.

Seed is plentiful, but the results are variable, and may be quite different from the parent; vegetative propagation takes up more room and may be slightly slower, but gives it consistently similar results to the parent.

Vegetative propagation

This is by far the most common means of propagation for indoor plants, and it includes propagation by cuttings (stem, leaf, and root), division, layering, offsets, plantlets, and air layering. Each technique relies on using part of the parent plant to produce the new one, without necessarily detaching it first. The offspring is genetically identical to the parent, and its growth pattern should also be identical.

Cuttings

Taking a cutting means removing part of the parent plant in order to grow the new one. Once the piece is severed, its supply of moisture from the parent's roots is cut off, so an adequate level of moisture has to be maintained within the cutting while it produces its own roots.

Some plants produce roots so easily that the cutting can be placed in a container of water. Others need help

Part-leaf cutting

1 *Leaves can be cut along the length of the central vein (midrib).*

2 *Lay the leaf down lengthways, pressing the cut edge lightly into the moist compost.*

3 *New plants should form along the cut edge. These can be planted individually.*

from a rooting hormone—in either liquid or powder form—to produce roots.

Spring and summer are the best times to take cuttings of all types, because the plant is actively growing and light levels are high. Avoid taking cuttings when the plant is in flower because flowering shoots will not root successfully, wasting compost, time, and the cutting.

Stem cuttings

The formation of roots is triggered when hormones in the cutting respond to stress. These plant hormones are concentrated in the growing tip but are also found in each leaf node. The younger the plant, the greater the chance that almost any part of the stem will root if there is a leaf node present.

Stem: Some plants root so well that a growing tip on the cutting is not necessary. From a long shoot it is possible to take the tip cutting; then cut the rest of the stem into similar lengths, making each top cut just above a leaf node, and each bottom cut just below.

Tip: Remove the end of a shoot including the growing tip and at least 3–4 in. (7–10 cm) of stem. Trim the cut

> ### ROOTING HORMONE
>
> Rooting hormone (powder or liquid) mimics natural plant hormones and boosts the rooting process. Not all plants need it; for instance, *Pelargoniums* tend to rot if it is applied. The powder is powerful, and is needed only on the cut surface itself—the very end of the cutting should be dipped into the powder and tapped gently as it is lifted away to get rid of the surplus.

end under a leaf joint, and remove the leaves from the lower third of the cutting. Dip the very end of the cutting in rooting hormone and tap off the surplus. Insert the cutting into a pot of moist compost by pushing it in to ensure good contact between stem and mix.

Heel: Short sideshoots of 3–4 in. (7–10 cm) long can be taken as tip cuttings. Pulling them from the stem, complete with a "heel" of bark attached. This strip should be trimmed down to a short point to prevent rotting.

Cane: Plants such as *Cordyline*, *Dieffenbachia*, *Dracaena*, and *Yucca*, which form strong, woody stems, can be propagated by cutting one of their bare stems into several pieces, each 2–3 in. (5–7 cm) long.

Whole-leaf cutting

1 *Whole leaves of succulents, such as Crassula and Sedum, can be used to form new plants. Take a large, healthy leaf and let it dry for 24 hours before planting to reduce moisture lost by excessive "bleeding."*

2 *Push the cut end of the leaf into the moist soil mix, but do not cover the pot. Begonia rex can be propagated by taking a whole leaf and making slits through each of the main veins.*

3 *The leaf is then weighed or pegged down to ensure it remains in good contact with the sterile potting mix.*

Self-propagating plants

Plants like *Chlorophytum* and *Tolmiea* produce small replicas of themselves on long stems or mature leaves as they grow. These replicas are complete with tiny roots that are ready to start growing as soon as they come into contact with compost. They can be rooted while still attached to the parent plant or separated, potted, and grown with a minimum of fuss as they establish. In fact, the only difficulty may be with the sheer quantity of offspring produced, although there is no actual need for them to be removed, and they can remain on the plant indefinitely. If the plantlet already has roots, it can be detached and rooted in water or small pots of compost right away, because these roots will only take a few days to begin supporting the plant.

Bulblets

Many plants that arise from bulbs reproduce themselves as miniature bulbs as well as by seed. The small bulbs are much quicker to reach maturity than by seed and lack the variation. Those that arise in the leaf axils on the stem are known as bulbils; those that arise at the base or are cultivated by breaking the scales, from a lily bulb, are bulblets.

1 *Remove healthy scales from a tiny bulb and place in a bag of moist compost. Keep warm and dark for 8–10 weeks.*

2 *Tiny white bulblets with delicate roots will form on each scale.*

3 *Scales can be cut lengthways to give separate bulblets, each with a piece of scale for food.*

4 *Plant into fresh compost. The first-year leaves will resemble grass. Flowering takes 3–4 years.*

Division

1 This technique is suitable for any indoor plant that forms a clump as it grows, including Chamaedorea, Maranta, Saintpaulia, Sanseveria, cacti, orchids, and ferns. Remove the plant from its pot and lay it on a flat surface to examine it. Select a point where separation looks possible and gently begin to tease the roots apart.

2 It may be necessary to wash the roots to get a clearer view, but it is important to inflict as little damage as possible to the roots, because it will hinder recovery. Plants with a rhizomatous or very dense root system may need the help of a knife, so make sure it is clean and sharp and the cut is made in as few movements as possible. For the greatest chance of success, each piece of plant should have both leaves and roots.

3 The new plants can be planted into separate pots slightly larger than their root system, and watered to settle the potting compost around the roots.

Offsets

No offset should be severed from the parent plant until it is large enough to survive on its own. Although this is not always easy to judge, they can generally be taken once they resemble the parent plant in shape and characteristics. They may even develop roots of their own before they are severed, which makes success even more likely.

Use a sharp, clean knife to cut the offset from as close to the parent as possible and place it into a pot of moist potting compost. Larger offsets may be unsteady, and need supporting with short canes until the roots provide firm anchorage.

Gently wash the plant roots.

Aloe variegata with several offsets.

Seed

Unlike plants grown from cuttings, which are clones of the parent, those grown from seed can bear characteristics of ancestors going back several generations rather than just the parents, so that the exact appearance of the offspring is hard to predict.

It is less common to grow indoor plants from seed than outdoor varieties, because far more are produced than can normally be used, although the surplus can always be given away or swapped. The attraction becomes the chance to grow something exotic, such as an avocado, lychee, or citrus, from a seed that might otherwise be discarded. This can also be an easy way to interest a child in the process of growing. For the avid cook, it is also easy to grow sprouting beans and herbs like basil and parsley from seed in a succession of small useable batches to ensure a regular, manageable supply.

Sowing fine seed

The easiest way to handle really fine seed is to mix it with light-colored sand before sowing, so it can be seen. As with any seed, always be guided by the instructions on the seed packet regarding the depth at which to plant the seed and whether it should be covered. If there is no packet, the general rule is that the smaller the seed, the

Maintenance

Remove the covering once germination starts, and move the seed into bright light, but not direct sun. Turn regularly if the light is one-sided, to prevent the seedlings becoming drawn and bent. As soon as the young plants have two true leaves (which appear after the first "seed" leaves) they can be "pricked-off" into small, individual pots of compost. Handle by the leaves at this stage, not the stem, because bruising the stem now will kill the plant. Settle by watering gently, rather than pressing the compost with fingers or a dibber, because this can damage the roots.

Use a dibber to transplant seedlings.

less covering it needs, and the very finest seed may not need to be covered at all. Cover the pot with a plastic bag, held tightly in place with an elastic band, or place a sheet of glass over the seed tray, and place it in a shady spot at a temperature of 60–70°F (15–20°C).

1 Fill a pot or seed tray with soil mix and level it roughly.

2 Use a board to firm the soil mix very gently.

3 Sieve a fine layer of soil mix on top to form the seedbed.

4 Sprinkle pinches of sand/seed mixture evenly over the soil mix.

Sowing small seed

Some plants can be raised indoors purely for the fun of it and the feeling of satisfaction gained from the sight of a new shoot emerging from the compost. Citrus seed falls into this category, especially for children, because the seed is free, would otherwise be thrown away, and germinates very quickly to produce an attractive plant with fragrant, glossy leaves. It is unlikely to produce fruit but citrus plants are worth growing for the foliage alone.

1 *Sow the seeds fresh from the fruit.*

2 *Press them gently into the soil mix.*

3 *Water, then keep warm and moist.*

Sowing large seed

Large seeds can be sown in pots.

The main advantage large seed has over smaller seed is the ease with which it can be handled, because it does not need mixing with sand or thinning out if too many seedlings germinate. In fact, large seeds can usually be sown into individual pots of compost large enough to support their growth for several weeks, thus eliminating the need to transplant the seedling and risk it suffering a check in growth as a result of the shock.

Coconut is the largest seed grown for indoors, but these are already germinated when they are bought. Avocado and date stones fall into the same category as citrus, in that the seed would otherwise be discarded, so there is nothing to lose by sowing them. Both can be soaked in water before sowing to maintain the moisture level inside the seed.

Spores (ferns)

Select a mature frond with sporangia showing on the underside and check the ripeness of the spores by touching gently—a dustlike deposit on the finger indicates that they are ready.

Spores on the back of a fern leaf.

Detach the frond with a clean, sharp knife and lay it face-up on a piece of clean white paper. Keep in a warm place for a day or two, so plenty of spores are shed. Sow the spores onto moist, sterile compost, enclose in a plastic bag, and place in a warm position with bright light, but not direct sun. Mist spray twice a week with water—boiled and allowed to cool—until the compost is covered with green "moss" (6–12 weeks). Prick out small pieces of "moss" onto sterile compost and mist with lukewarm boiled water, seal into plastic bags, and keep warm and well-lit, misting daily. Tiny ferns will develop that can be transplanted when larger.

Basket of azaleas

Arranging houseplants

The size of the display you create with your plants will be governed by the space you wish to fill. The critical point to consider as you design your display is scale. Too small a display within its setting, and the effect will be lost. Too large, and the effect will be too overwhelming.

Most flowering plants look best when they are massed together in a group, either with identical plants or an assortment of different varieties that all require the same growing conditions. Foliage plants can also be massed together. Choose plants with similar leaf color or go for contrasting shades.

Single specimens

If you are going to fill a small space with a single specimen, choose a plant with dramatic foliage, such as a *Begonia rex* hybrid, and set it in a complementary container that will not draw attention away from the beautiful leaves.

Alternatively, look for a plant with an abundance of attractive flowers, such as *Rhododendron simsii* (azalea) or *Pericallis* x *hybrida* (florist's cineraria), that is suited to the particular situation.

Try to celebrate the seasonal changes by using an attractive, red-bracted poinsettia (*Euphorbia pulcherrima*) or a pot of spring bulbs, such as tulips, fragrant hyacinths, or dwarf narcissus.

To make a dramatic statement with a single specimen, choose a large plant that features architectural foliage, such as *Chamaedorea elegans* (the parlor palm) or the brightly colored *Solenostemon* 'Kong'. Depending on the choice of plant, the container can be selected to recede into the background—

plain terra-cotta, green, or gray—or be part of the display in its own right (decorated terra-cotta, metal or color coordinated with the decor).

Groups of plants

Grouping plants together is the ideal way to make a big impact, even if your group of plants is small. A collection of plants in a wide bowl on a low table will make a greater impression than a single plant in the same place.

Flaming Katy (*Kalanchoe blossfeldiana*) can be brought into flower at any time of the year.

A wrought-iron chair in a greenhouse makes a great home for this group of foliage plants that combines leaf color, shape, and form.

You can choose a selection from a particular genus, such as a begonia with its colorful leaves, or from a specific type of plant, such as desert cacti. The main requirements of the plants have to be considered as you make your selection, as well as the positioning of the display. Mixing cacti and ferns, for instance, will cause problems because each needs an entirely different growing environment. One way to make sure you can still deal with each plant individually is to leave each in its own pot within the display and simply place it into another sort of medium. This also allows you to replace any individual specimen that performs poorly or a flowering centerpiece after blooms fade.

On a larger scale, you can plant troughs or large containers in the same way, using plain green or white-variegated foliage plants to act as a foil to brighter colors or flowers.

Individual containers can be positioned together as a group, particularly on a terrace or balcony, or in the garden room to give a long-lasting display. You can vary the display by bringing colorful plants to the fore, then retiring them farther back as they pass their season of interest, or replacing the main focal point regularly with a colorful flowering specimen.

Grouping plants together is beneficial for the plants because it allows them to form their own small micro-climate. Evaporating moisture is trapped under the leaves, raising the humidity in the plants' immediate environment and making growing conditions more favorable.

Mixed pelargoniums

Architecture and plants

Plants can be used to echo, define, and complement the architecture or layout of your home. The nature of the planting will be defined by the style of the setting. A formal design will demand a similarly precise display, while a relaxed setting allows for a much softer planting.

Strong, straight vertical lines can be echoed by using tall, upright plants such as *Cocos nucifera* or *Sansevieria trifasciata,* but they can also be softened by using plants such as *Licuala grandis*, with large, rounded leaves marked by long, straight veins.

Spiky plants such as *Yucca filamentosa* and the *Dracaena* species have such strong, definite lines that they are ideal in a formal setting, as are plants such as *Hedera* (ivy) when trained around tall metal frames.

Steps or a staircase can provide the opportunity to create a neatly regimental display of plants with a single pot on each step. In a formal setting, this could be exactly the same plant, at the same size, and in identical pots. Ideally, use nonflowering plants for this, because it is difficult to keep flowering ones at the same stage.

In a less formal setting, steps are ideal for fragrant plants such as spring bulbs that you will pass regularly and appreciate the scent. You could also use herbs or scented-leaf *pelargoniums*, particularly in a garden room or leading to a veranda.

Single large specimen plants can be used to echo horizontal lines in masonry, windows, and furniture as well as vertical ones. Many large-leaved plants, such as *Ficus elastica, Fatsia japonica,* and x *Fatshedera lizei,* have leaves that spread horizontally. Smaller, softer-looking

ARCHITECTURE AND PLANTS

Anthurium scherzerianum FLAMINGO FLOWER. Inflorescences (flowers) are its most striking feature.

Asparagus spp. Grown for their graceful, soft foliage.

Caladium bicolor Heart-shaped, impressively colored leaves.

Chrysalidocarpus lutescens ARECA PALM. Attractive, arching fronds providing rain-forest effect in a sunroom setting.

Cocos nucifera COCONUT PALM. Great specimen plant.

Cyperus papyrus EGYPTIAN PAPER REED. Large, clump-forming plant.

Dieffenbachia maculata Striking feature plant, either on its own or in a massed arrangement.

Fatsia japonica Impressive specimen plant.

Ficus spp. Use as a centerpiece for mixed planting.

Howea forsteriana Excellent indoor specimen plant, but provide sufficient space.

Licuala grandis Long-stalked leaf blades, makes an impressive feature plant.

Nolina recurvata BOTTLE PALM. Clusters of long, dark green leaves are at the top of a flask-shaped trunk that is swollen at the base.

Phoenix canariensis CANARY ISLAND DATE PALM. Decorative palm tree, ideal for sunroom.

Polyscias guilfoylei May be too large for the house, but excellent in a warm sunroom.

Rhapis excelsa LADY PALM. Spectacular as an indoor specimen.

Schefflera spp. Umbrella-like leaf formation.

Yucca filamentosa Stout stem with sword-shaped leaves.

The different forms of *Ficus*, such as *F. benjamina* (right), can be used to good effect around the home.

plants such as *Ctenanthe oppenheimiana* and *Dieffenbachia seguine,* with their definite angular growth habit, are also complementary to strong horizontal lines and geometric angles in the home.

The ultimate opposite to the strong, straight line is the "fluffy" plant, such as *Cyperus papyrus, Chamaedorea elegans,* or *Chrysalidocarpus lutescens.* These all look like foliar explosions and are perfect for softening harsh lines. Used alone or in conjunction with a larger display, they give a lush, tropical effect that can be instantly relaxing.

Creating "walls"

As mentioned earlier, plants can have a beneficial effect on our environment, increasing the oxygen in the air and absorbing the toxins given off by furniture and electrical equipment, so it makes good sense to incorporate them wherever possible.

In the home we tend to think of using plants as punctuation points, on tables or windowsills, but they can also be used to mark zones within the living area. Positioned on furniture units, they can extend the height upward; standing on the floor, they are a mobile wall; and hanging from the ceiling, they can become a living wall where none existed before.

Because it is becoming increasingly common for people to work from home for at least part of their week, the new wall can be used to delineate between "work space" and "home space" or simply between the relaxing and dining areas in an open-plan home.

The size of the plants used will be dictated by their purpose. The job of a "mobile wall" will be best filled by a single large specimen, while the plants to be used on furniture or hanging from the ceiling or over shelves will be smaller.

This tall *Ficus binnendijkii* has long spiky stems that offer attractive visual interest.

Plant Directory

Whether you are still trying to choose the right plant for your home or have already chosen one and now need advice on caring for it, this section will help provide valuable information. Each plant entry gives a description, cultural information, and details of how to propagate it, if appropriate. Icons (see below) give you at-a-glance information on individual plant care. They indicate, where appropriate, the height, spread, room temperature, and type of light needed for each plant.

Remember that the closer you suit a plant to its environment, the better it will thrive and the more you can enjoy it.

Average height of plant

listed if the plant is over 4 in./10 cm tall.

Average width of plant

provided if the plant is more than a single-stemmed climber.

Preferred temperature

normal or average equals to 60–70°F (15–21°C)

cool is 55–65°F (12–18°C)

warm is above 65°F (18°C) at all times

frost-free means above 40°F (5°C) during winter

Amount of light required

Abutilon x *hybridum* 'Bella Vanilla'
Flowering maple

14–18 in.
(35–47 cm)
high

Cool but
frost-free:
45–60°F
(7–15°C)

Full sun
or indirect
sunlight

This is a striking flowering plant that can be raised quite easily from seed. It will flower during its first season, producing large, open, bell-shaped blooms approximately 3 in. (7.5 cm) in diameter, with a large golden central stamen. Each flower lasts only about 2 days, but each is produced in succession. The plant will tolerate bright sun or partial shade and is happy in a range of temperatures, although the flower color tends to be slightly better in cooler temperatures. The wide, light green leaves are smaller than most other abutilons, making the flowers seem even larger.

Caring for plants
Keep the potting soil moist at all times and use standard liquid fertilizer every 2 weeks during the flowering season.

Making new plants
Sow seed in a sterile medium and cover with Vermiculite. Keep at 72–75°F (22–24°C) until germination, which should be in 3–5 days. Plant the seedlings into pots quickly to allow each plant room to branch. From sowing to first flowering should only be about 12 weeks.

Abutilon x *hybridum* 'Bella Vanilla'

Achimenes erecta (syn. *A. coccinea*)
Cupid's bower, Nut orchid, Magic flower

| To 18 in. (47 cm) high | 60–80°F (15–25°C) | Indirect sunlight |

This is a trailing achimenes despite its name. It can produce a spectacular display of flowers and foliage. It grows from small rhizomes, each of which sends up one reddish green stem carrying pairs of heart-shaped, dark green, and hairy leaves. The bright red flowers last for only a few days but are produced over a period lasting from June to October. This variety grows well in a hanging basket in a warm, well-lit place, or it can be made to bush by tying the stems to short canes and pinching the shoots regularly.

Caring for plants
Keep the potting mix thoroughly moist throughout spring to autumn, but do not water at all during the winter. Water with standard liquid fertilizer every 2 weeks during spring to autumn. Achimenes can tolerate temperatures as low as 55°F (12°C), but not above 80°F (25°C) or the buds will shrivel and die.

Making new plants
Take tip cuttings or pieces of rhizome around 3 in. (7.5 cm) in length in spring to summer and plant in a sterile medium in individual pots.

Achimenes erecta (syn. *A. coccinea*)

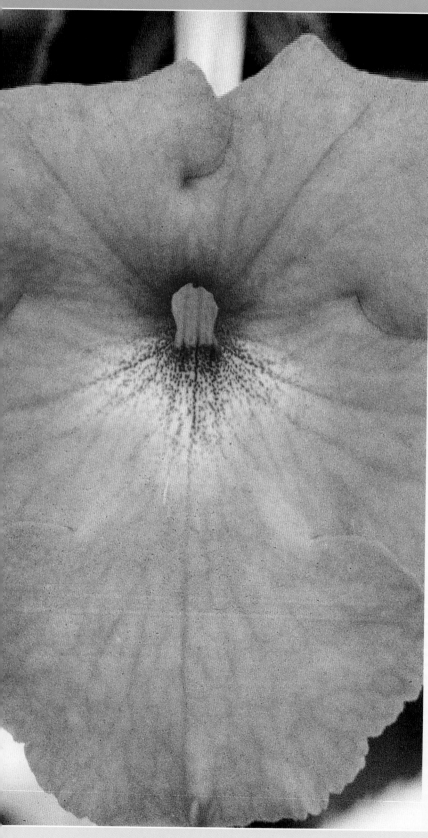

Achimenes longiflora
Cupid's bow, Nut-orchid, Magic flower

To 24 in. (60 cm) high

60–80°F (15–25°C)

Indirect sunlight

*A*chimenes *longiflora* has trailing stems up to 24 in. (60 cm) long, arising from small rhizomes. The hairy leaves have saw-toothed edges and are up to 3½ in. (8 cm) long and 1½ in. (4 cm) wide. The flowers are produced from June to October and are blue with a white throat. They are quite large—up to 2 in. (5 cm) long and 3 in. (7.5 cm) across. There is a form with pure white flowers—*A. longiflora* alba— and a hybrid—*A. longiflora* 'Ambroise Verschaffelt'—that has white flowers with purple lines running down the throat.

Caring for plants
Keep the potting mix thoroughly moist during spring to autumn; then gradually reduce the amount of water. Do not water at all during the winter. Water with standard liquid fertilizer every 2 weeks during spring to autumn. Achimenes can tolerate temperatures as low as 55°F (12°C), but not above 80°F (25°C) or the buds will shrivel and die.

Making new plants
Take tip cuttings or pieces of rhizome around 3 in. (7.5 cm) long in spring to summer. Pot in a sterile medium in individual small pots.

Achimenes longiflora

Adiantum pedatum
Five-fingered maidenhair fern, American maidenhair fern

Up to
24 in.
(60 cm)
high

Normal-
warm room
temperature,
minimum
50°F (10°C)

Indirect
sunlight

This is an uncommon but extremely attractive maidenhair fern, differing from others in the shape of the 12-in. (30 cm)-long frond blades, which are almost palmate. They are carried on leafstalks up to 20 in. (50 cm) long. The small leaflets (pinnules) are oblong and pale green. All maidenhair ferns need warmth and humidity in order to thrive. *Adiantum pedatum* 'Japonicum' (Early red maidenhair) has fronds up to 12 in. (30 cm) in length, which are purple-pink as they first emerge. *A. pedatum* 'Laciniatum' has fronds to 8 in. (20 cm) in length, and the pinnules are deeply divided.

Caring for plants
Keep the potting soil moist at all times and water with half-strength liquid fertilizer once a month in spring to summer. Adiantums like high humidity but not wet roots, which will quickly begin to rot, and they should never be allowed to dry out. Drafts and dry air will cause the leaves to shrivel and die.

Making new plants
Either divide older clumps or remove a small piece of rhizome with 1 or 2 fronds attached.

Adiantum pedatum 'Laciniatum'

Adiantum raddianum
Maidenhair fern

| 18 in. (47 cm) high | 24 in. (60 cm) spread | 60–70 °F (15–20 °C) | Indirect sunlight |

This is the most popular fern for growing indoors. It gets its common name because the shiny dark leafstalks resemble human hair. The dark green, triangular fronds are semierect at first, drooping gracefully as they age, and can be up to 8 in. (20 cm) long by 6 in. (15 cm) wide. This is a pretty, delicate plant in its own right but complements, fills, and softens when added to other arrangements. To grow well, it needs moist air, warmth, and shade and will prefer to live in a greenhouse or bathroom rather than the living room or hallway.

Caring for plants
Keep the potting mix moist, but do not allow it to become waterlogged. Ferns cannot thrive if they are neglected. They need both moist air and compost; dry air, gas fumes, and cold drafts will harm them, as will allowing the soil mix to dry out and then soaking it. Remove older fronds as their appearance deteriorates, a few at a time from right at their base in spring each year to allow space for new shoots to develop. This fern also benefits from monthly fertilizing throughout the growing season.

Making new plants
Divide older clumps in spring or break off new clumps from the rhizome with 1 or 2 fronds attached. Plant in potting soil in individual small pots.

Adiantum raddianum

Aechmea fasciata
Urn plant

To 36 in.
(90 cm)
high

Normal room
temperature
(min. 60°F/15°C)

Direct
sunlight

Aechmeas naturally live as epiphytes on the branches of trees, rooting into accumulated debris. They need little support and get all their moisture by catching rain in their rosettes of leaves. The arching, spiny leaves are grayish green in color, with powdery white cross markings and can reach 24 in. (60 cm) in length. Each rosette produces 1 flower spike as it matures, carrying pink bracts that surround the tiny flowers, which are pale blue at first but rapidly turn red. The flowers themselves are short-lived, but the 6-in. (15-cm) inflorescence can remain decorative for several months. After flowering, the rosette slowly dies, to be replaced by new offsets.

Caring for plants

Water regularly to keep the soil moist but not wet. The central reservoir of water should never be allowed to dry out, but it should be emptied and refilled periodically to prevent the water from becoming stagnant. Hard tap water will mark the leaves so it is preferable to use rainwater to fill the central cup. Feed into both the central cup and the compost every 2 weeks during spring and summer.

Making new plants

Detach the new offsets once they are half the size of the parent plant and pot in a fine soil mix in a medium-sized container.

Aechmea fasciata

Aeonium arboreum 'Zwartkop'
No common name

24 in.
(60 cm) high

24 in.
(60 cm) spread

Normal
room
temperature

Indirect
sunlight

This is an upright, succulent subshrub that has long been popular in frost-free areas as a striking plant for an outdoor container, but it is now increasing in popularity as an unusual indoor or greenhouse feature. It looks equally impressive in a container on its own or used to contrast with brighter-colored foliage or flowers. Each basal branch produces a tightly packed rosette of narrow, spoon-shaped leaves, edged with fine hairs. They are a striking dark, glossy, purple-black color, shading to emerald green at the base, giving each rosette a green center. Older plants will produce large, pyramid-shaped clusters of yellow flowers in spring, up to 12 in. (30 cm) tall.

Caring for plants
Keep the medium moist at all times but not wet, and give standard liquid fertilizer once a month during the growing season. If the plant is kept in too dark a position, the leaves will become more green. In direct sunlight behind glass, they may scorch.

Making new plants
Take smaller rosettes as cuttings in early summer. Root in barely damp cactus mix and place in good light.

Top and bottom: *Aeonium arboreum* 'Zwartkop'

Aeschynanthus speciosus
Basket plant

Trailing stems
to 24 in.
(60 cm)

Normal room
temperature

Indirect
sunlight

There are many species of *Aeschynanthus*, all of which have long, trailing stems and bright, striking flowers. The large, fleshy, dark green leaves are up to 4 in. (10 cm) long and 1½ in. (4 cm) wide, and are arranged in threes along the stems, although there tends to be a cluster of 4 to 8 at the end of the stem surrounding the base of the cluster of flowers. The flower cluster consists of 6–20 flowers, each flower surrounded by a short yellow-green calyx. The flowers may be as long as 4 in. (10 cm) and are shaded in color from orange-yellow in the lower part to orange-red at the tip, with blotched dark red inside and a yellow-streaked throat.

Caring for plants

Water plentifully during flowering. At other times keep medium thoroughly moist. High humidity is essential, so mist daily—especially when in flower. If the growing conditions are warm and moist, your aeschynanthus will not have a rest period, so watering will be required constantly all year. Water with one-eighth-strength standard liquid fertilizer at every watering.

Making new plants

Take tip cuttings 4–6 in. (10–15 cm) long at any time, and root in a sterile medium. Aeschynanthus prefers an acid soil mix.

Aeschynanthus speciosus

Aglaonema crispum (syn. A. roebelenii)

Aglaonema crispum (syn. *A. roebelenii*)
Painted drop tongue, Chinese evergreen

To 36 in. (90 cm) high

Normal room temperature

Cool light

An attractive and long-lived plant, aglaonema can eventually become large specimen plants. The leaves are thick and leathery, growing to 12 in. (30 cm) long and gray-green-edged olive in color. The variety *Aglaonema crispum* 'Silver Queen' has dark gray-green leaves heavily marked with silvery white and cream. The flower is not particularly showy and consists of a spathe with a central spadix produced in summer or early autumn. As the plant ages, it tends to form a stout trunk, scarred by old leafstalks, with a cluster of 10–15 leaves at the top. This can be disguised by grouping with other plants.

Caring for plants
Keep thoroughly moist during spring to autumn and slightly drier in winter. Water with standard liquid fertilizer once a month in spring to summer.

Making new plants
With a sharp knife, sever a basal shoot bearing 3–4 leaves and preferably some roots at a point just below soil level in spring. Transplant and keep enclosed in a plastic bag. Rooting should take 6–8 weeks.

Allamanda cathartica
Golden trumpet

Up to
20 ft (6 m) high

Warm,
min 60°F
(15°C)

Direct
sunlight

This vigorous climbing plant is probably best suited to a warm greenhouse, where it can grow to its full height or be trained against a wall, although it can also easily be trained to a support or frame. The leaves are a glossy dark green, oval in shape, and 4–6 in. (10–15 cm) long. The flowers are produced throughout the summer and are a spectacular golden yellow, marked white in the throat. Other varieties include *Allamanda cathartica* 'Grandiflora', which has more compact, large flowers, *A. cathartica* 'Hendersonii', which has buds tinged bronze and orange-yellow flowers; and *A. cathartica* 'Nobilis', which has very large bright gold flowers and large, glossy leaves.

Caring for plants
Keep the potting soil moist during spring to autumn, but allow it to dry slightly in winter. Water with standard liquid fertilizer every 2 weeks in spring to summer. This is quite a strong-growing plant, so it can be cut down by two-thirds in winter.

Making new plants
Take tip cuttings 3–4 in. (7.5–10 cm) long in spring, pot in a sterile medium, and cover with a plastic bag or place in a propagator. Keep the cuttings at 21°C (70°F), in bright light but not direct sun.

Allamanda cathartica

Allium schoenoprasum

Allium schoenoprasum
Chives

12 in.
(30 cm) high

Around
60°F (15°C)

Bright
position

Chives are members of the onion family and are perennial, clump-forming herbaceous plants with hollow, grasslike leaves and mauve flowers. Although they are commonly grown outdoors in a herb garden, they may be grown indoors for winter use. The leaves are chopped and are used for garnishing soups, cream cheeses, and dips, and the edible flowers brighten salads. Both the leaves and the flowers can be used fresh, or the young leaves can be frozen or dried.

Caring for plants
Keep in a humid atmosphere and water regularly. They will need regular misting in high temperatures. To maintain humidity, plants can be grouped together with other herbs on trays of moist pebbles. Remove flower heads for a continuous supply of fresh leaves.

Making new plants
Sow seed for fresh plants, or divide established clumps in spring.

Aloe vera
Aloe

To 36 in.
(90 cm)
high

Normal room
temperature

Direct
sunlight

Aloe vera has become popular since its increased use in medical preparations and because the direct application of juice from a snapped-off leaf is reputed to relieve the pain of a burn. Perhaps this is a plant everyone should keep at home. It grows as a rosette of gray-green succulent leaves, which are usually tinged red and are sometimes spotted. The edges of the leaves are pale pink and toothed. The flower spike grows to 36 in. (90 cm), and the tubular yellow flowers are 1¼ in. (3 cm) long.

Caring for plants
Water plentifully from spring until autumn, then sparingly in winter. Fertilize with full-strength liquid fertilizer every 2 weeks from spring until autumn. Check for pests regularly, because mealy bugs are inclined to hide in the folds of the rosette.

Making new plants
Detach suckers with a sharp knife, as close to the parent plant as possible, as soon as they begin to open into a rosette shape.

Aloe vera

Alternanthera 'Purple Knight'
No common name

| 15–20 in. (40–50 cm) high | 24–36 in. (60–90 cm) spread | Normal to hot room temperature | Full sun or indirect sunlight |

This is a striking plant grown for its impressive dark purple leaf color. It is very tolerant, ideal for growing in a mixed container or display, where the dark foliage can be used to full effect on its own or as a foil among other plants. Its growth is fairly vigorous in the ground, but less so in a container, where the roots are more restricted. It has a branching-upright-and-spreading habit, which can be encouraged by regular pinching while the plant is young. This plant will thrive in a hot summer.

Caring for plants
Keep the soil mix moist at all times but not wet, and give standard liquid fertilizer once a month during the growing season. Foliage color is darkest in full sun.

Making new plants
Sow seed in a germinating soil mix and cover with Vermiculite. Keep at 72–75°F (22–24°C) until germination in 3–5 days. Pot quickly to allow individual plants room to branch.

Alternanthera 'Purple Knight'

Ananas bracteatus var. *tricolor*
Red pineapple

36 in. (90 cm) high	36–60 in. (90–150 cm) spread	Needs to be constantly warm to produce edible fruit	Direct sunlight

Pineapples ultimately grow into very large plants, so they are only suitable for use indoors for a few years. In a heated greenhouse, they will last until they outgrow their allotted space. They are dramatic plants with rosettes of long, sharply toothed leaves striped with cream and they are flushed and edged with pink. The fruit forms on a 12–18-in. (30–47-cm)-long stalk and is green-brown in color surrounded by red bracts. Unless the growing conditions are ideal, it may not be edible.

Caring for plants
Keep the potting mix moist at all times, but not wet. Pineapples like high humidity, so stand the pot on a tray of damp pebbles and mist regularly. Water with standard liquid fertilizer at every watering.

Making new plants
Detach offsets when they are 4–6 in. (10–15 cm) long, and root in a sterile medium. Rooting should take about 8 weeks.

Top and bottom: Ananas bracteatus var. tricolor

Ananas comosus var. *variegatus*
Pineapple

36 in.
(90 cm)
high

20 in.
(50 cm)
spread

Needs to be
constantly above
65°F (18 °C)
to produce
edible fruit

Direct
sunlight

This highly ornamental form of pineapple is a ground-growing bromeliad with tightly packed rosettes of slightly curved, spiny-edged leaves up to 36 in. (90 cm) long. They are dark green with creamy yellow margins, sometimes flushed rosy pink. In the right summer conditions, a flower will be produced, with around 12 in. (30 cm) of small, reddish yellow bracts enclosing violet-blue flowers, sometimes followed by a bright red fruit of a similar size.

Caring for plants
Keep moist at all times, but not wet, and water with standard liquid tomato fertilizer at half strength at every watering. The fruit is edible—it is a close relative of commercial varieties—but may be tough and fibrous if it grows too slowly.

Making new plants
Detach offsets when they are 4–6 in. (10–15 cm) long. They should root in a sterile mix in about 8 weeks.

Ananas comosus var. variegatus

Anthurium scherzerianum
Flamingo flower, Tailflower

| Up to 24 in. (60 cm) high | 18 in. (47 cm) spread | Warm, preferably 65-70°F (18-20°C) | Indirect sunlight |

The most striking feature of this anthurium is its long-lasting flowers or inflorescences, which consist of a thin, twisted, orange-red spadix 2–3 in. (5–7.5 cm) long, surrounded by a flat scarlet spathe 3–4 in. (7.5–10 cm) long. The flowers usually appear from February to July, although plants growing in good conditions may produce more throughout the year. The leaves are dark green, leathery, lance-shaped, and up to 8 in. (20 cm) long. They mix well among other plants. Other forms include: *Anthurium scherzerianum* 'Atrosanguinium', which has a deep red spathe; *A. scherzerianum* 'Rothschildianum', with a red spathe spotted white and a yellow spadix; and *A. scherzerianum* 'Wardii', which has red stems, a large, dark burgundy spathe, and a long red spadix.

Caring for plants

Keep the potting mix thoroughly moist from spring to autumn, but allow it to dry slightly between waterings during the winter. High humidity will encourage the plant to flower more prolifically. If the flower stems start to flop, tie them to thin stakes pushed in around the sides of the pot. Water with liquid fertilizer every 2 weeks during spring to autumn.

Making new plants

Large clumps can be divided in spring; each section will need a growing point and some roots. Transplant and keep at a steady 70°F (20°C) until growth starts.

Anthurium scherzerianum

Aphelandra squarrosa 'Louisiae'
Zebra plant, Saffron spike

12–18 in. (30–47 cm) high	12 in. (30 cm) spread	Normal room temperature. Winter min. 55°F (12°C)	Indirect sunlight

This plant could be grown for its attractive foliage alone, so the bright yellow flower comes as a bonus. The leaves are a glossy dark green color, with vivid white markings along the midrib and veins. They are 8–10 in. (20–25 cm) long. The flowers—which are usually on the plant when it is purchased—are a brilliant golden yellow, and this earns the plant its common name. The actual flowers are fairly short-lived, but the surrounding bracts last long after the flowers have gone.

Caring for plants
Keep the soil mix thoroughly moist during spring to autumn. During winter the plant is resting, so allow the top half of the mix to dry between waterings. Aphelandras like high humidity, so set the pot in a tray of moist pebbles. Water with standard liquid fertilizer weekly during spring and summer.

Making new plants
Take tip cuttings 4–6 in. (10–15 cm) long during spring to summer. Root in a sterile medium in individual pots.

Aphelandra squarrosa 'Louisiae'

Argyranthemum— Madeira series
Marguerite

12–14 in.
(30–35 cm)
high

12–14 in.
(30–35 cm)
spread

Normal
room
temperature

Indirect
sunlight

This attractive, compact plant with its wide, daisylike flowers and divided, matte green foliage, is a wonderfully colorful addition to any indoor display. Unlike its larger predecessors, which originated as garden plants, the new *Argyranthemum* Madeira series has been developed with indoor and greenhouse use in mind. There are 11 varieties in the series, including 'Santana' (rose-red with a yellow center), 'Machio' (double, pink), and 'Sao Martinho' (anemone-form, creamy white). They will flower profusely throughout the summer and thrive in a cooler situation, as long as they have good light. They actually produce better flower colors in slightly lower temperatures.

Caring for plants
Keep the soil moist at all times. Water with standard liquid tomato fertilizer at half strength every 2 weeks from spring to late summer. Pinch growing tips when the plant is young to produce a bushier plant.

Making new plants
Best treated as an annual and replaced each year.

Other varieties
Argyranthemum foeniculaceum has pretty white daisy flowers with yellow disk florets in the center. It needs good light, but it is happy with cooler temperatures, making it ideal for use in a garden room. *Argyranthemum (Chrysanthemum) frutescens* is a bushy plant with deeply cut blue-gray leaves and masses of flowers covering the plant in either yellow or white.

Argyranthemum—Madeira series Top, '*Machio*', Bottom, '*Porto Santo*'.

Asparagus densiflorus 'Sprengeri'
Emerald fern

Stems can reach to 39 in. (100 cm) in height

Normal room temperature

Indirect sunlight

This is a delicate, fernlike plant, with woody stems that can be erect or trailing. The feathery emerald green foliage is prized by flower arrangers, but it is also useful among a group of other indoor plants to soften the display and add contrast. The flowers are small and insignificant but are sometimes followed by bright red fruits. Although the term "fern" appears in the name, these are not true ferns and are actually in the lily family.

Caring for plants
Keep the soil mix thoroughly moist during spring to autumn, but during the winter, give only sufficient water to prevent drying out. Water with standard liquid fertilizer every 2 weeks during spring to autumn. Keep out of direct sun, which will scorch the foliage.

Making new plants
Divide larger plants in spring and repot the individual clumps.

Asparagus densiflorus 'Sprengeri'

Asparagus setaceous (plumosus)
Asparagus fern

Stem height can be as much as 48 in. (120 cm) Normal room temperature Indirect sunlight

Despite the common name, this plant is not a true fern, but its delicate foliage does resemble that of a fern and is often used by florists in bouquets. The stems are green and wiry and will naturally climb or scramble as the plant matures. The bright green "leaves" are actually modified branchlets, which form flattened triangular-shaped sprays. The misty effect of the foliage means that this is an ideal plant for softening and filling in an arrangement, particularly where it has room to follow its natural growth habit.

Caring for plants
Keep thoroughly moist during spring to autumn, but during winter apply only sufficient water to prevent drying out. Water with standard liquid fertilizer every 2 weeks in spring to autumn. Keep out of direct sun, which will scorch the foliage.

Making new plants
Divide larger plants in spring, and transplant the individual clumps.

Asparagus setaceous (plumosus)

Aspidistra elatior
Cast-iron plant

18 in.
(47 cm)
high

24 in.
(60 cm)
spread

Tolerant of a
wide range of
temperatures

Partial
shade

The aspidistra is one of the most resilient houseplants ever introduced. It is tolerant of bad light, gas fumes—hence its popularity in Victorian times—and even extreme temperatures. It grows as a clump, producing many single dark green leaves that reach lengths of up to 24 in. (60 cm). The cream and purple flowers are produced in spring and are 1 in. (2.5 cm) long, but may not be seen among the foliage.

Other forms include *Aspidistra elatior* 'Milky Way', which has leaves speckled with white; *A. elatior* 'Variegata', with variegated cream leaves; and *A. elatior* 'Variegata Exotica', which has leaves very boldly streaked with white.

Caring for plants
Aim to keep the soil mix barely moist at all times. Overwatering causes brown blotches on the surface of the leaves. Water with standard liquid fertilizer at each watering.

Making new plants
Divide large plants in spring; each piece should have both leaves and some roots. Plant in a humus-rich soil mix in individual pots.

Aspidistra elatior

Asplenium nidus
Bird's nest fern

  24 in. (60 cm) high　　 **36 in. (90 cm) spread**　　 **Not below 60°F (15°C)**　　**Indirect sunlight**

This true fern takes its common name from the arrangement of its leathery, apple green leaves, which form an open rosette. Unlike many ferns, the leaves are uncut and may reach 48 in. (120 cm) in length—although they are usually about 18 in. (47 cm) long by 2–3 in. (5–7.5 cm) wide. New leaves uncurl from the central, fibrous brown core, and for the first few weeks they are quite delicate, so they should not be handled. Brown blotches on the reverse of older fronds are likely to be spore cases rather than insects, particularly if they are arranged in a regular pattern.

Caring for plants

Keep the potting soil thoroughly moist. Mature fronds will benefit from having dust gently wiped away at regular intervals. Water with standard liquid fertilizer once a month during spring to autumn.

Making new plants

Propagation is by spore—which is difficult to achieve. Offsets are not formed.

Asplenium nidus

Begonia x *hiemalis*
Winter-flowering begonia

| 18 in. (47 cm) high | 12 in. (30 cm) spread | Normal room temperature | Indirect sunlight |

Although the common name of this plant suggests that it flowers only in the winter, improvements in breeding mean that it is now available in flower all year round. It is fibrous-rooted with single or double flowers. It ranges in color from white to pink, yellow-orange, or red. The leaves are usually a glossy pale green, but plants with darker-colored flowers also tend to have darker, more bronzy foliage. This group of begonias was previously known under the name of *Begonia* x *elatior* or the 'Elatior' hybrids.

Caring for plants
Keep the potting soil moist, but not wet—overwatering can cause rotting. Water with standard liquid fertilizer every 2 weeks during spring to summer. Keep out of direct sunlight, which can cause scorching on the leaves.

Making new plants
Take tip cuttings 3–4 in. (7–10 cm) long from nonflowering shoots, and root in a sterile medium.

Other varieties
Begonia bowerae is a bushy, stemless plant grown for its attractive foliage rather than its flowers, which are small and pale pink. High humidity is important, so stand the pot on a tray of moist pebbles and mist regularly. Good hygiene is critical where humidity is high, because gray mold thrives in such conditions.

Begonia x *hiemalis*

Begonia x *hybrida* 'Baby Wing Pink' Begonia

12–15 in. (30–40 cm) high	15–18 in. (40–47 cm) spread	Normal room temperature	Full sunlight (protect from midday summer sun behind glass) to indirect sunlight

This is an "angel wing" begonia, named for the unusual triangular-to-oval shape of each glossy, almost succulent-looking leaf. The growth is lush and vigorous, and the plant is easy to grow, making it ideal for filling a container with bright color. It is one of the earliest begonias in the year to flower, with its pretty, nodding blooms held above the foliage. The flowers are small and light pink, with rose-colored buds. This plant is extremely heat and stress tolerant, and although it likes bright light, it will tolerate partial shade. It has a multibranching habit, so there is no need to pinch the growing tips.

Caring for plants

Keep the soil mix thoroughly moist at all times. Water with standard liquid fertilizer at half strength every 2 weeks during the spring and summer.

Making new plants

Sow seed in a germinating mix, and do not cover. Keep at 72–75°F (22–24°C) until germination in 7–10 days. Pot quickly to allow individual plants room to branch. The plants are directional and should be planted with the growing shoot facing outward toward the edge of the container.

Other varieties

Begonia x *hybrida* 'Dragon Wing' is also an "angel wing" begonia. The large, somewhat pendulous blooms are bright scarlet with golden anthers in the center.

Top and bottom: Begonia x hybrida 'Baby Wing Pink'

Begonia rex
Painted-leaf begonia

| 12 in. (30 cm) high | Up to 36 in. (90 cm) | Normal room temperature | Indirect sunlight |

*B*egonia rex and its closely related hybrids in the Cultorum group have the most dramatic foliage of any of the begonias. They are rhizomatous, with large, puckered leaves, which can be hairy both on top and underneath. The leaves of *Begonia rex* are a rich, metallic green splashed with silvery white above and dull red beneath. The leafstalks are red and hairy, and the winter-borne flowers are pink. The Cultorum group of hybrids is large, with most plants being grown for their foliage rather than their flowers. The leaves are heart-shaped, up to 12 in. (30 cm) in length, and have striking patterns in a range of colors including wine red, shades of green, bronze, and silver.

Caring for plants
Keep the soil moist, but not wet; overwatering can cause rotting. Water with standard liquid fertilizer every 2 weeks in spring to summer. Keep out of direct sunlight, which can cause scorching on the leaves.

Making new plants
Take 2–3-in. (5–7.5-cm)-long sections of rhizome, each with a growing point, plant them shallowly, and cover with a plastic bag. Alternatively, take leaf cuttings by cutting a healthy leaf at an angle of 45° from the plant, with 1-2 in. (2–3 cm) of leafstalk attached. Plant in a pot or tray of soil mix and enclose it all in plastic. Transplant when the small new plantlets have 2–3 leaves.

Begonia rex

Billbergia nutans
Friendship plant, Queen's tears

Up to 24 in.
(60 cm)
high

Normal
room
temperature

Direct
sunlight

*B*illbergia nutans is one of the easiest of the
bromeliads to grow and is a popular and an
attractive indoor plant. The arching, olive green
leaves reach a length of about 18 in. (47 cm)
and form a rosette, although the prolific
production of offsets means that the overall
appearance is grasslike. Each flower spike
carries a cluster of small pink, blue, and yellow-
green flowers, backed by long pink bracts.

Caring for plants
Keep the potting soil thoroughly moist all year.
Water with standard liquid fertilizer every 2
weeks in spring and summer. After a rosette has
flowered, it should be cut away to allow the
surrounding offsets to develop.

Making new plants
Remove 4–6-in. (10–15-cm)-long offsets in
spring, plant shallowly in small pots, and allow
to root—this should take 6–8 weeks.

Billbergia nutans

Blechnum gibbum
Miniature tree fern

| 48 in. (120 cm) high | 36 in. (90 cm) spread | Warm, preferably above 60°F (15°C) | Indirect sunlight |

This is a large fern that will tolerate a certain amount of dry air indoors. The fronds are carried in a rosette and can be either sterile or fertile, reaching 36 in. (90 cm) long by 12 in. (30 cm) wide. The shiny green pinnae are slightly drooping. As it grows, a scaly black trunk develops, which can be as long as 36 in. (90 cm), and gives rise to the common name.

Caring for plants
Keep the potting soil thoroughly moist at all times. If the temperature falls below 55°F (12°C) in winter, reduce watering to a minimum. Water with half-strength liquid fertilizer once a month from spring to summer. To maintain adequate humidity, stand the pot on a tray of moist pebbles.

Making new plants
Detach and transplant offsets if they are produced. Otherwise, it is possible to propagate from spores.

Blechnum gibbum

Bougainvillea glabra
Paper flower

  Up to 10 ft (3 m) high

 Not less than 50°F (10°C) in winter

Direct sunlight

Bougainvilleas are woody, spiny plants, which originate in the subtropical areas of South America and need high levels of both warmth and light in order to flourish. They are also vigorous growers, although regular pruning and training will keep them smaller and more bushy. Given good conditions, they will produce their vividly colored bracts—which surround the insignificant cream flowers—in clusters of 10–20 throughout the spring and summer. The bracts are in shades of white, pink, red, or purple.

Other varieties include *Bougainvillea glabra* 'Variegata', which has gray-green leaves splashed with cream; *B. glabra* 'Magnifica', with vivid purple bracts; and *B. glabra* 'Sanderiana', which has long-lasting magenta bracts.

Caring for plants
Keep the soil thoroughly moist from spring to autumn but apply only enough water to prevent drying out in winter. Water with standard liquid fertilizer every 2 weeks from spring to summer. Leaf loss in winter is normal, but at any other time it indicates that all is not well in terms of growing conditions. To reduce excessive growth, cut long shoots back to 2–3 buds in early spring and reduce the rest of the growth by one-third.

Making new plants
Take tip cuttings 6 in. (15 cm) long in spring, transplant and place in a heated propagation case. Rooting should take 6–8 weeks.

Bougainvillea glabra

x *Brassolaeliocattleya* hybrids
Orchid

| 18 in. (47 cm) high | 18 in. (47 cm) spread | Normal room temperature. Winter min. 55°F (12°C) | Indirect sunlight |

This group of spectacular hybrids arose from crosses between *Brassavola, Cattleya,* and *Laelia* orchids. The pseudobulbs that make up the body of this epiphytic plant are stout and club-shaped, each producing 1 or 2 semirigid, oval-to-lance-shaped, straplike leaves with a leathery texture. The large, fragrant, brightly colored flowers are produced in spring or autumn from the sheaths of the leaf bases. Each flower lasts for up to 4 weeks and is up to 7 in. (18 cm) across, singly or in clusters of up to 3 blooms. The hybrid 'Sweet Honey' has large butterfly-shaped flowers of bright candy pink with a yellow center.

Care of plants
Water freely from spring until autumn; then apply only enough water to prevent the soil mix from drying out. Water with standard liquid fertilizer once a month during spring and summer. Plants should be grown in epiphytic orchid compost.

Making new plants
Divide the mature plant when it outgrows its pot, potting the pseudobulbs separately.

Top and bottom: x *Brassolaeliocattleya* hybrids

Browallia speciosa
Bush violet

18–24 in.
(47–60 cm)
high

55–60°F
(12–15°C)

Direct sunlight,
except at midday
in summer

A glorious display of large sapphire blue flowers in autumn and winter makes browallia an impressive and attractive potted plant. The trailing stems lend themselves to use in a hanging basket, and by removing the flowers as they fade, the display can be prolonged for several weeks. It is best treated as an annual and discarded once flowering is over. *B. speciosa* 'Major' has a more upright habit, bright green leaves, and large violet-blue flowers with a white throat and deep blue veining on the petals. *B. speciosa* 'Silver Bells' is a white form.

Caring for plants
Keep the soil mix moist at all times. Water with standard liquid fertilizer every 2 weeks while the plant is in flower. The thin branches need tying to stakes if the plant is to be grown as a bush. Higher than recommended temperatures will make the flowers fade quickly.

Making new plants
Sow seed in germinating mix in spring or summer. Pinch out the tips of the shoots as they grow to make them bush.

Browallia speciosa

Brunfelsia pauciflora 'Macrantha'
Yesterday, today, and tomorrow

Up to 24 in. (60 cm) high	12 in. (30 cm) spread	Normal room temperature all year to maintain flowering	Direct sunlight, except midday in summer

The fascinating common name of this shrub comes from the coloration of the flowers, which open purple, change to violet, and finally turn white over a period of about 3 days. They are flat, up to 3 in. (7.5 cm) across, and are produced in clusters of up to 10. Grown in good conditions, brunfelsia can become a bushy plant of up to 24 in. (60 cm) in height, producing flowers throughout the year, but it must be in a position away from sudden temperature changes in order to achieve this.

Caring for plants
Keep the soil mix thoroughly moist at all times. Water with standard liquid fertilizer every 2 weeks. High humidity is important, so stand the pot on a tray of moist pebbles and mist regularly. Old plants can be pruned hard in spring. Take out up to half of the existing stems and pinch the resultant new growth to make it bush.

Making new plants
Take tip cuttings 3–4 in. (7–10 cm) long in spring and summer, and root in a sterile medium.

Brunfelsia pauciflora 'Macrantha'

Caladium bicolor
Angel wings, elephant's ear

Leaves up to 18 in. (47 cm) long, total height up to 24 in. (60 cm)

Warm, at least 65–75°F (17–23°C)

Indirect sunlight

The caladiums are a large group of tuberous-rooted plants with strikingly colored, paper-thin, heart-shaped leaves that rise on long, fleshy stalks directly from the base. Leaf color and size varies considerably between the different hybrids, and they look particularly attractive when they are grouped together or mixed with other foliage plants. *Caladium bicolor* 'White Queen' has white leaves with crimson veins and green edges; *C. bicolor* 'Carolyn Whorton' has pink leaves, with green-black marbling, and red ribs; *C. bicolor* 'Gingerland' has gray leaves with white ribs, maroon spots, and dark green edges; and *C. bicolor* 'Miss Muffet' is a dwarf form, with sage-green leaves with white ribs and a soft red center.

Caring for plants

Keep the potting soil thoroughly moist in spring to summer, but reduce watering through the rest period to a minimum just to prevent the medium from drying out. Water with half-strength liquid fertilizer every 2 weeks during spring to summer. In order to thrive, caladiums need a five-month rest period starting when the leaves die down in autumn and lasting until the following spring.

Making new plants

As the plant emerges from its rest period, small tubers can be detached from the parent plant and potted.

Caladium bicolor

Calathea makoyana
Peacock plant, Cathedral windows, Brain plant

39 in.
(100 cm)
high

24 in.
(60 cm)
spread

Warm,
60–70°F
(15–20°C)

Indirect
sunlight

Although this tropical plant produces white flowers surrounded by green bracts, they are of minor importance compared to the dramatic foliage. The oval-shaped leaves can be as long as 13 in. (33 cm) and are a pale green in color, feathered cream with dark green blotches along the veins and a dark green edge. Underneath, they have the same pattern, but it is shaded with purple.

Caring for plants
Keep the soil mix thoroughly moist in spring to autumn and slightly drier in winter. In warmer temperatures, increase the humidity by misting daily with rainwater—to avoid marking the foliage. Bright light will cause the leaf markings to fade. Water with standard liquid fertilizer every 2 weeks in spring to summer.

Making new plants
Divide mature plants in spring; each clump needs roots and shoots to grow. Enclose the new plant in a plastic bag to keep the humidity high until it has rooted.

Calathea makoyana

Calceolaria—
Herbeohybrida group
Slipper flower, Pouch flower

18 in.
(47 cm)
high

Cool,
50–60°F
(10–15°C)

Indirect
sunlight

These plants flower gloriously for several weeks in spring, but are best regarded as short-term plants for indoors and discarded once flowering has finished. The inflated, pouch-shaped flowers come in shades of white, yellow-orange, copper, and red, and most are blotched with other colors. The soft and bushy leaves grow up to 8 in. (20 cm) across and are clustered at the base of the plant.

Caring for plants
Keep the potting soil thoroughly moist at all times. It is not necessary to fertilize this plant. Watch for aphids, which love the lush growth, and keep them shaded from bright sun, which will scorch the leaves.

Making new plants
Sow seed in summer in a cool environment for flowering the following year. It is not easy to get the seed to germinate, so it is probably best to buy starter plants at your local nursery.

Calceolaria—Herbeohybrida group

Calliandra haematocephala
Powder puff

| 36 in. (90 cm) high | 36 in. (90 cm) spread | Normal to cool room temperature | Direct sunlight (shade from midday summer sun) |

This attractive plant is ideal for the greenhouse, porch, or garden room because it will eventually form a rounded bush. It has dark, glossy green leaflets, arranged in pairs along a central leafstalk. The flowers are produced on the shoot tips in summer and look like fluffy balls due to the prominent stamens, which are white at the base, turning deep red. Forms with pink or white stamens are also available.

Caring for plants
Water freely from spring until autumn; then apply only enough water to prevent the medium from drying out. Water with standard liquid fertilizer once a month during spring and early summer. If it is necessary to keep the size restricted, prune in late winter or early spring.

Making more plants
Take semiripe cuttings in summer, and root in a sterile starting medium.

Top and bottom: *Calliandra haematocephala*

Callistemon citrinus
Bottle brush

36 in. (90 cm) high	36 in. (90 cm) spread	Cool room temperature	Direct sunlight

This attractive shrub is quite hardy in the warmer parts of the world but it is ideal for the garden room or porch elsewhere, as long as the light is good. During the summer months it can be moved outdoors. It has slender, arching branches with narrow, dark green leaves. The flowers form brilliant, crimson-red spikes on the end of the shoots in spring and summer. The stamens circle the shoot, giving rise to the common name. These are followed by small, acornlike seed cases.

Care of plants
Water freely from spring until autumn; then apply only enough water to prevent the soil mix from drying out. Water with standard liquid fertilizer once a month during spring and early summer. Growth continues beyond the flower, leaving a bare patch, so prune immediately after flowering, shortening the shoot to below the bare part. This plant will tolerate hard pruning.

Making more plants
Take semiripe cuttings in summer, and root them in a sterile starting medium.

Callistemon citrinus

Camellia japonica
Camellia

Variable, up
to 45 ft.
(15 m) high

Cool,
between
45–60°F
(7–15ºC)

Indirect
sunlight

Camellias are large shrubs or small trees that will survive all but the very harshest winters outdoors in Zones 8–10, as long as they are growing in the acid conditions they prefer. They can be grown under cover, where they will benefit from protection against the weather, but they need a cool, light, airy position, such as an unheated greenhouse or porch. The leaves are a glossy dark green, and the flowers come in a range of colors from white to dark red. Varieties are available with single, semidouble, and double flowers, produced from late winter until summer, according to variety.

Caring for plants
Keep the potting soil thoroughly moist at all times and water with standard liquid fertilizer every 2 weeks during spring to summer. Since they are essentially outdoor plants, it is preferable to bring camellias indoors only while they are in flower, unless they can be kept cool.

Making new plants
Take semiripe cuttings in summer, with at least 1 in. (2.5 cm) of brown, woody stem at the base. They will need rooting hormone and bottom heat—an electric propagation case would be ideal.

Top and bottom: *Camellia japonica*

Campanula isophylla
Star of Bethlehem, Falling stars, Italian bellflower

Stems up to
12 in.
(30 cm)
high

Normal room
temperature or
cooler, winter
min. 45°F (7°C)

Indirect
sunlight

A pretty, trailing form of campanula that looks equally good tumbling from a pot or hanging basket, the star-shaped flowers are produced throughout summer and autumn. They are usually violet-blue, although *Campanula isophylla* 'Alba', a white form, and *C. isophylla* are also available. There is also a double form, *C. isophylla* 'Flore Pleno'. The stems and leaves of campanula are bright green and slightly brittle. If they are broken, they exude a distinctive smell and a milky-white sap.

Caring for plants
Keep the potting soil thoroughly moist during spring to autumn but slightly drier in winter. Water with standard liquid fertilizer every 2 weeks from late spring to autumn. Removing flowers as they fade helps to prolong the flowering period. Once flowering has finished in autumn, cut the stems back hard, close to the base.

Making new plants
Take tip cuttings 2 in. (5 cm) long in spring and root in cutting medium or water.

Campanula isophylla

Canna x *generalis*
Canna lily

24–48 in.
(60–120 cm)
high

Warm,
70–80°F
(20–25°C)

Indirect
sunlight, some
direct sunlight

Cannas have tall, erect flower spikes carrying exotic blooms, which come in a wide variety of colors ranging from white to red through yellow and pink. They can be plain, striped, or spotted. The plant makes a bold, cheerful addition to an indoor display, particularly in a warm position. The leaves, arising from the rhizomatous root system, are long and straplike, ranging from gray and leathery to chocolate red and thin. *Canna* x *generalis* 'Black Knight' has brown leaves and red flowers, *C.* x *generalis* 'Lucifer' is a dwarf form with green leaves and crimson flowers with yellow borders, and *C.* x *generalis* 'Orchid' has deep pink flowers.

Caring for plants
Keep the soil mix thoroughly moist during spring to autumn, but reduce watering through the winter to a minimum just to prevent the mix from drying out. Water with standard liquid fertilizer every 2 weeks from summer to autumn. If the temperature is very high, mist regularly.

Making new plants
Divide the rhizomes in spring and transplant individually.

Canna x *generalis*

Capsicum annuum
Ornamental pepper

12 in. (30 cm) high	Normal room temperature	Indirect sunlight, some direct sunlight

These are among the few indoor plants grown for their fruits rather than their flowers or leaves. The tiny white flowers in summer or autumn are followed by the attractive fruits, which are green, turning to orange, red, or purple over a period of weeks as they ripen. There are a number of different fruit shapes, including the cherry pepper 'Christmas cherry', which is ball-shaped, and the cone pepper, which is conical and upright. These plants are particularly popular at Christmas.

Caring for plants
Keep the potting soil thoroughly moist at all times and water with a standard liquid fertilizer every 2 weeks. Be sure to wash your hands thoroughly after touching the fruit—these are relatives of chili and cayenne peppers, so they are extremely hot and will make the eyes and mouth sting if the juice comes into contact with them.

Making new plants
Sow seed in early spring. It is difficult to achieve new plants successfully.

Capsicum annuum

Cattleya
Orchid

| 12–36 in. (30–90 cm) high | 10–12 in. (25–30 cm) spread | Normal room temperature. During winter rest, keep at about 60°F (15°C) | Indirect sunlight |

These are a group of evergreen epiphytic orchids that produce pseudobulbs on short rhizomes. The leaves are leathery, semirigid, and mid- to dark green, produced singly or in pairs. The flowers are large and showy, with 3-lobed or entire central "lips." They are borne singly or in clusters at the ends of the shoots, and there are hundreds of hybrids to choose from, in colors ranging from white through yellow, gold, orange, pink, mauve, and purple to shades of green. There is often a contrasting flush of color on the lips.

Caring for plants
Grow in fine-grade epiphytic orchid medium in a container or slatted basket. From spring to autumn, water and mist daily. In winter, water sparingly. Water with standard liquid fertilizer once a week.

Making new plants
Divide the mature plant when it fills the pot, and transplant the separate parts.

Top: *Cattleya* hybrid; Bottom: *Cattleya skinneri*

Cereus (peruvianus) uruguayanus
Peruvian apple cactus

Up to
15 ft. (5 m)
high

Normal room
temperature.
Winter min.
50°F (10°C)

Direct
sunlight

This is a dark green, columnar cactus with 5–9 thick ribs and few branches. The ribs are rounded with 8–9 stout yellow or reddish brown spines growing from brown areoles. Nocturnal, widely funnel-shaped white flowers up to 6 in. (15 cm) long are produced in summer. The outer petals may be tipped green-brown or red.

Caring for plants
Keep the soil mix moist—but never wet—during spring to autumn, but in winter apply only enough water to prevent the compost from drying out. Water with half-strength liquid tomato fertilizer once a month during spring to summer. Give the plant as much direct sun as possible all year to encourage it to flower.

Making new plants
Sow seed at 66–75°F (19–24°C) in spring, or take cuttings of young branches in late spring or early summer. Root cuttings in a sterile medium in individual pots.

Cereus (peruvianus) uruguayanus

Chamaedorea elegans
Parlour palm

Up to 36 in.
(90 cm)
high

Preferably
warm, 65–75°F
(18–25°C).
Winter min.
55°F (12°C)

Indirect
sunlight

One of the most popular indoor palms, this plant has graceful, arching leaves that can grow up to 24 in. (60 cm) in length from a short central stem. These darken from medium to glossy dark green as the plant ages, and the mature plant occasionally produces sprays of small yellow flowers. The variety *Chamaedorea elegans* 'Bella' reaches to only half this height and is often the plant on sale for indoors.

Caring for plants
Keep thoroughly moist during spring to autumn, but during winter apply only sufficient water to prevent the soil mix from drying out. Humidity is important, so stand the pot on a tray of damp pebbles. Water with half-strength liquid fertilizer once a month in spring to autumn.

Making new plants
It is not practical to take cuttings or grow from seed—buy small new plants instead.

Chamaedorea elegans

Chlorophytum comosum
Spider plant, Ribbon plant

Up to
24 in.
(60 cm)
high

Normal
room
temperature

Indirect
sunlight

The spider plant is a dramatic trailing plant when set in a hanging basket or on a pedestal, where it can grow unhindered. This effect is enhanced by the long, curved, straplike leaves, and arching stems bearing tiny white flowers or numerous small plantlets. *Chlorophytum comosum* 'Vittatum' has green leaves with a broad white stripe running lengthwise down the center, *C. comosum* 'Picturatum' has a yellow central stripe, and *C. comosum* 'Variegatum' is green at the center and white or cream at the edges.

Caring for plants
Keep the soil mix thoroughly moist during spring to autumn but slightly drier in winter. Allowing the plant to dry out will result in permanent brown tips on the leaves. Water with standard liquid fertilizer every 2 weeks from spring to autumn.

Making new plants
Young plantlets can be rooted in water or potting soil either before or after being detached from the parent. If they are in water, transplant as soon as the roots are 1 in. (2.5 cm) long.

Chlorophytum comosum

Chrysalidocarpus lutescens
Areca palm, Yellow palm

Up to 60 in.
(150 cm)
high
in 10 years

Normal
room
temperature

Indirect
sunlight

The waxy stems of this dramatic palm grow in clusters, producing yellowish green fronds that are first upright, then gradually arch over as the feathery green leaflets unfurl. Mature fronds can be up to 84 in. (210 cm) long, with up to 60 leaflets (pinnae) on either side of the midrib (rachis). Growth is slow, with only about 8 in. (20 cm) added each year to even the best-positioned plants. The remains of old fronds leave the stem marked like bamboo canes. This plant needs space but gives an instant jungle effect in a warm greenhouse or sunroom.

Caring for plants

Keep the soil thoroughly moist at all times, but reduce watering to a bare minimum if the temperature falls below 55°F (12°C). Water with standard liquid fertilizer every 2 weeks from spring to autumn.

Making new plants

Remove suckers in spring, ideally about 12 in. (30 cm) long with plenty of roots. Plant in a fast-draining soil mix.

Chrysalidocarpus lutescens

Cissus antarctica
Kangaroo vine

Up to
10 ft. (3 m)
high

Normal
room
temperature

Indirect
sunlight

This woody vine is a relative of the grape and has a similar pattern of growth—it forms long, trailing stems that can support themselves with curling tendrils. This allows it to be used in a wide variety of ways, from being trained up a wall or trellis to cascading out of a large hanging basket. The glossy, heart-shaped leaves are 3–4 in. (7.5–10 cm) long, toothed, and pointed, and produced on red-tinted petioles. *Cissus antarctica* 'Minima' is a dwarf, slow-growing form with spreading branches.

Caring for plants
Keep the soil mix just moist during spring to autumn. In winter, apply only sufficient water to prevent drying out. Water with standard liquid fertilizer every 2 weeks from spring to autumn. Pinching out the growing tips regularly will produce a more bushy plant.

Making new plants
Take tip cuttings 4–6 in. (10–15 cm) long in spring. Use rooting hormone, and transplant in a sterile starting medium.

Cissus antarctica

Cissus rhombifolia
Grape ivy, Venezuela treebine

Up to
10 ft. (3 m)
high

Normal
room
temperature

Indirect
sunlight

This is a vine with lush, glossy foliage that quickly grows to form a striking feature. The trailing stems support themselves by using forked tendrils, allowing it to be grown up a wall or trellis or, alternatively, trailed from a hanging basket. The glossy, toothed leaves are carried as 3 rhomboid leaflets. Fine white hairs cover the new growth, giving it a silvery sheen, and the older leaves are covered underneath with fine brown hairs. *Cissus rhombifolia* 'Ellen Danica' has larger, circular leaflets.

Caring for plants
Keep the soil mix just moist during spring to autumn. In winter, apply only sufficient water to prevent drying out. Water with standard liquid fertilizer every 2 weeks from spring to autumn. Pinching out the growing tips regularly will produce a more bushy plant.

Making new plants
Take tip cuttings 4–6 in. (10–15 cm) long in spring. Use rooting hormone and root in a sterile starting medium.

Cissus rhombifolia

x *Citrofortunella microcarpa* (formerly *Citrus mitis*)
Calamondin orange

48 in.
(120 cm)
high

Normal room
temperature.
Winter min.
50°F (10°C)

Direct
sunlight

This is a popular ornamental orange that produces fruits when it is still quite young. The leaves are a glossy dark green, and the small, fragrant white flowers are produced intermittently throughout the year. Small, round oranges follow so that unripe green fruits are carried at the same time as bright orange ripe ones. Although bitter, they are useful for making marmalade. x *Citrofortunella microcarpa* 'Tiger' has leaves that are edged and streaked with white.

Caring for plants
Keep the potting soil moist during spring to autumn. In winter, apply only sufficient water to prevent the mix from drying out. To increase the humidity, stand the pot on a tray of moist pebbles. In warmer areas, the plants can be placed outdoors during the summer months. Pinch the growing tips at regular intervals. Water with liquid tomato fertilizer every 2 weeks in spring to autumn.

Making new plants
Take tip cuttings 4 in. (10 cm) long in spring to summer, preferably semiripe with a heel, and dip them in hormone rooting powder. Also sow seed from the fruits, although these will take longer to grow to flowering size.

x *Citrofortunella microcarpa*

Citrus limon
Lemon

| Up to 84 in. (210 cm) high | Normal room temperature. Winter min. 50°F (10°C) | Direct sunlight |

Lemons ultimately grow into small trees, but while they are young, they make attractive indoor plants, producing flowers and fruit intermittently all year when conditions are right. They have glossy, deep green, oval-shaped foliage and spiny stems. The flowers are white tinged with purple and fragrant, with 5 blunt petals and large stamens. Each fruit ripens slowly from green to yellow, so that there will be fruit of various sizes and color shades on the plant at the same time. Their palatableness depends on the variety. To grow edible fruit of a good size, choose a named variety. *Citrus limon* 'Variegata' has variegated cream leaves, and fruit that is striped green before it becomes fully yellow.

Caring for plants
Keep moist during spring to autumn. In winter, apply only sufficient water to prevent the mix from drying out. To increase the humidity, stand the pot on a tray of moist pebbles. In warmer areas, the plants can be placed outdoors during the summer months. Pinching the growing tips at regular intervals will produce bushy growth. Fertilize with citrus fertilizer every 2 weeks from spring to autumn.

Making new plants
Take tip cuttings 4 in. (10 cm) long in spring to summer, preferably semiripe with a heel, and dip in hormone rooting powder before rooting in a sterile medium. Also sow seed from the fruits, although these will take longer to grow to flowering size.

Citrus limon

Clerodendrum thomsoniae
Bleeding-heart vine, Glory bower

Up to 10 ft. (3 m) high

Normal room temperature, cooler in winter (50–55°F or 10–12°C)

Indirect sunlight

This is a vigorous, twining shrub with long, weak stems, which can rapidly become straggly if not trained against a support or pinched regularly to make the plant more bushy. The large, coarse leaves are heart-shaped and dark green with pronounced paler veins. Clusters of up to 20 flowers are produced in summer. Each consists of a white, bell-shaped calyx over a red, star-shaped corolla.

Caring for plants
Keep thoroughly moist during spring to autumn. In winter, apply only sufficient water to prevent the mix from drying out. Extra humidity in summer will help flowering, so stand the pot on a tray of moist pebbles. To keep the plant under control, cut the stems back by up to two-thirds as growth starts in spring. Water with standard liquid fertilizer every 2 weeks in spring to autumn.

Making new plants
Take tip cuttings 4–6 in. (10–15 cm) long in spring and dip in hormone rooting powder before rooting in a sterile medium. Keep enclosed in a plastic bag or heated propagator at a temperature of 70°F (21°C). Rooting will take 4–6 weeks.

Clerodendrum thomsoniae

Clianthus puniceus
Lobster claw

72 in. (180 cm) high	36 in. (90 cm) spread	Normal room temperature	Direct sunlight

This is an evergreen shrub with climbing shoots and dark green leaves divided into small leaflets. The unusual flowers are produced from spring into summer, are bright red, and reach up to 3 in. (7.5 cm) long. They grow in hanging clusters. The shape resembles the claw of a lobster; hence, the common name. White- and pink-flowered forms are also available. This plant looks equally attractive when trained up a support or allowed to trail from a raised container.

Caring for plants
Keep moist from spring until autumn; then apply only enough water to prevent the soil mix from drying out. Water with standard liquid tomato fertilizer at half strength every 2 weeks from spring to late summer. This plant grows best with really good drainage, so add extra sand or perlite to the soil mix.

Making new plants
Take semiripe cuttings in summer, and root in a sterile medium in individual pots.

Clianthus puniceus

Clivia miniata
Kaffir lily

36 in.
(90 cm)
across
spread

Normal
room
temperature

Indirect
sunlight

Dark green leaves that grow to a length of 24 in. (60 cm) make this an impressive indoor plant even when it is not in flower. But keep in mind that it does need space to develop. It should not be moved while the flowers are maturing or when they open. The 18-in. (47-cm) flower stalk appears in spring, carrying up to 15 broadly funnel-shaped flowers, each bright scarlet with a yellow throat and up to 3 in. (7.5 cm) long.

Caring for plants
In order to flower, it is important that this plant has a winter rest period of 6–8 weeks at 40–50°F (5–10°C). Not observing the winter rest results in short, premature flowers or a shortened flower life. Keep moist during spring to autumn. In winter, keep almost dry until the flower stalk appears, then increase watering. Water with standard liquid fertilizer every 2 weeks from when the flower stalk is 4–6 in. (10–15 cm) high until autumn. Clivias do not need repotting annually—only when they have completely filled their pot and the roots appear on the surface of the medium (every 3–4 years). Remove any fruits, which will sap so much of the plant's energy that they will reduce flowering the following year.

Making new plants
Divide the mature plant or detach offsets immediately after flowering, taking care not to damage fleshy roots. Root in a sterile medium in individual pots.

Clivia miniata

Cocos nucifera

Cocos nucifera
Coconut palm

60 in.
(150 cm)
or more
high

Warm

Indirect
sunlight

The coconut palm makes an interesting and unusual feature plant, either growing alone as a specimen or as a high point in a grouping. The trunk grows directly from the nut itself, which is partially buried in the soil mix, and the arching fronds have a sheath of woven, light brown fibers.

Caring for plants
Keep the potting mix moist at all times, and water with half-strength liquid fertilizer every 2 weeks during spring to summer. This plant has a limited life in the home because it resents root disturbance and, to grow well, it needs intense heat and high humidity, which is difficult to maintain.

Making new plants
This is not applicable in the home.

Cocos nucifera

Codiaeum variegatum
var. *pictum*
Croton, Joseph's coat

| Up to 36 in. (90 cm) high | Normal room temperature | Indirect sunlight, some direct sunlight (not midday in summer) |

The upward-pointing leaves of this tropical shrub are all glossy, leathery, and heavily patterned but vary widely in their size, shape, and color. They can be long and thin or broad and rounded, straight or twisted, entire or lobed. As the plant ages, the color of the leaves becomes more pronounced, in combinations of yellow, orange, pink, and red with glossy dark green. Small, insignificant cream flowers are also produced as the plant ages.

Caring for plants

Keep the soil mix thoroughly moist during spring to autumn. In winter, apply only sufficient water to prevent the mix from drying out. Increase humidity by standing the pot on a tray of moist pebbles. Water with standard liquid fertilizer every 2 weeks in spring to autumn. The stems exude milky sap when cut, so if a large plant needs trimming back, do it in early spring and put a small piece of paper tissue over the cut to absorb the latex.

Making new plants

Take tip cuttings in spring or summer, and dip in rooting hormone before rooting in a sterile medium.

Codiaeum variegatum var. pictum

Columnea gloriosa
Goldfish plant

Stems up to 36 in. (90 cm) long

Warm, 65–85°F (18–30°C)

Indirect sunlight

This is a dramatic plant for a high position or hanging basket, where the trailing stems—which can reach 36 in. (90 cm) long and branch only at the lower ends—can fully develop. Oval green leaves of up to 1 in. (2.5 cm) long are carried in pairs and all have a dense covering of red-purple hairs. The 3 in. (7.5 cm) flowers are borne singly in the leaf axils and are scarlet with a yellow throat.

Caring for plants
Water sparingly at all times, only enough to keep the soil mix barely moist. Water with liquid tomato fertilizer at one-quarter strength every watering during spring to autumn. Columneas are very susceptible to root rot, so both mature plants and cuttings need an open, free-draining medium. The foliage, however, needs high humidity and should be misted regularly with warm water—cold will mark the leaves.

Making new plants
Take tip cuttings 4 in. (10 cm) long in spring, and root in a sterile medium.

Columnea gloriosa

Cordyline australis
Cabbage palm

36 in.
(90 cm)
high

36 in.
(90 cm)
spread

Normal
room
temperature

Direct sunlight
for green-leaved
varieties. Indirect
sunlight for varieties
with colored foliage.

This is an upright specimen plant that would ultimately form a palmlike, woody-stemmed tree if space allowed. The spiky foliage is ideal for adding a focal point to a mixed planting, but it is just as attractive when used alone. The long, straplike leaves arch outward from a central tuft or rosette. They can reach 12–36 in. (30–90 cm) long and may be highly colored or striped. *Cordyline australis* 'Albertii' has matte green leaves with a red central midrib and pink edges, with cream stripes down each leaf. In summer, mature plants produce clusters of tiny creamy white, sweetly scented flowers, sometimes followed by white or bluish-tinted berries.

Caring for plants
Keep moist from spring to autumn. In winter, apply sufficient water to prevent the mix from drying out. Water with standard liquid fertilizer monthly from spring to late summer. Cordyline is generally trouble-free, but watch for scale insects and red spider mites.

Making new plants
Sow seed at 60°F (16°C) in spring, or alternatively, remove rooting suckers in spring.

Cordyline australis

Crassula ovata (was *C. argentea*)
Dollar plant, Jade plant, Jade tree

36–48 in.
(90–120 cm)
high

Cool to
normal room
temperature

Some direct
sunlight

Jade plants are many-branched shrubs, with thick, fleshy stems covered with peeling bark. The spoon-shaped leaves are shiny mid- to dark green, often with a horny, red or pale green marking around the edge. The small, star-shaped flowers are white tinged pink, with purple anthers, and are produced in autumn in clusters up to 2 in. (5 cm) across. The form *Crassula ovata* 'Basutoland' has pure white flowers, while *C. ovata* 'Hummel's Sunset' has leaves that are golden yellow, edged with red, that become green, edged with yellow and red as they age.

Caring for plants
During the winter rest, keep the temperature between 45–55°F (7–12°C). In spring to autumn, allow to dry slightly between waterings. In winter, apply only sufficient water to prevent the mix from drying out. Water with a standard liquid fertilizer once a month during spring to autumn. No crassula will flower without sunshine.

Making new plants
Take individual leaves or tip cuttings 2 in. (5 cm) long and root in water or potting soil in spring or summer.

Crassula ovata

Crocus
Crocus

8 in.
(20 cm)
high

Cool,
65°F
(18°C)

Direct
sunlight

Crocus corms are generally known as bulbs but they are actually solid stems from which a bud containing the leaves and flower emerges. They are normally associated with springtime in the garden, but there are a number of varieties that will grow very well indoors before then, giving color in the early months of the year when there is little else around. In order to get the best results indoors, choose varieties marked on the packaging as "indoor" types. These include the smaller-flowered *Crocus chrysanthus*, which flowers in January to February, the slightly later *C. vernus*, flowering in February, and the large-flowered Dutch hybrids, which flower February to March. The cup-shaped flowers come in a variety of colors, including purple, yellow, and white, and can be plain or striped. All have long, thin, green-and-white striped leaves.

Caring for plants
Keep the potting soil moist but not too wet. It is not necessary to fertilize; once the flowers begin to fade, remove just the flowers and continue watering, leaving the stem and leaves to die down gradually.

Making new plants
Unlike bulbs, corms do not flower a second time, but produce new corms from lateral buds. These can be detached and transplanted.

Crocus 'Jeanne d'Arc'

Cryptanthus bivittatus
Earth star

To 12 in.
(30 cm) in
diameter

Warm

Direct
sunlight

*C*ryptanthus is a genus of ground-dwelling bromeliads that naturally make their homes amid tree roots and in rock fissures. The dramatic foliage is rosette-forming, strongly marked, and highly colored, often with prickly edges. As air plants, they take little through their roots in the way of nutrients, using them chiefly for anchorage. The small white flowers are usually hidden in the leaves; hence, the Latin name, meaning "hidden flower." These stemless plants are ideal for growing in a bottle garden or terrarium. The leaves of *C. bivattatus* form a dense, spreading rosette and can reach 8 in. (20 cm) in length. They are sharply pointed and dark green, with two broad white or pink bands running along their length.

Caring for plants
Keep the potting soil barely moist at all times. Fertilize with only an occasional spray of half-strength foliar fertilizer to improve leaf coloration. After flowering has finished, cut away the parent plant to allow the new offsets to develop.

Making new plants
With a sharp knife, detach offsets in spring. These will root in a sterile medium in about 12 weeks.

Cryptanthus bivittatus

Cryptanthus bromelioides
Rainbow star

Height
to 18 in.
(47 cm)
high

Warm

Direct
sunlight

The dramatic foliage of cryptanthus is rosette-forming, strongly marked, and highly colored, often with prickly edges. Like other varieties, *Cryptanthus bromelioides* is a ground-dwelling bromeliad that grows naturally among tree roots and in rock fissures. It takes little through its roots in the way of nutrients, using them chiefly for anchorage. It grows upright rather than flat and spreads by means of stolons with plantlets at the ends. Its leaves are 4–8 in. (10–20 cm) long, olive green or variegated. The variety
C. bromelioides 'Tricolor' has leaves that are striped lengthwise with light green and cream, flushed rose pink in bright light. This is not one of the easiest plants to grow because it is inclined to rot at the base.

Caring for plants
Keep the potting soil barely moist at all times. Fertilize with only an occasional spray of half-strength foliar fertilizer to improve leaf coloration. After flowering has finished, cut away the parent plant to allow the new offsets to develop.

Making new plants
This variety of *Cryptanthus* produces plantlets that will root in a sterile medium in about 12 weeks.

Cryptanthus bromelioides

Cryptanthus fosterianus
Earth Star

Up to 20 in. (51 cm) high

(50 cm) in diameter

Warm

Direct sunlight

This is one of the largest species of *Cryptanthus*, with a flat rosette of thick, fleshy leaves that can reach up to 12 in. (30 cm) in length, in shades of copper green or purple brown, banded with gray. Like other varieties of bromeliads, it is stemless and takes in its nutrients through its leaves, using the roots mainly for anchorage. The Latin name means "hidden flower," because the small, white flowers are usually hidden in the leaves.

Caring for plants
Keep the potting soil barely moist at all times. Fertilize with only an occasional spray of half-strength foliar fertilizer to improve leaf coloration. After flowering has finished, cut away the parent plant to allow the new offsets to develop.

Making new plants
With a sharp knife, detach offsets in spring. They will root in a sterile medium in about 12 weeks.

Cryptanthus fosterianus

Ctenanthe oppenheimiana
Never-never plant

Up to
36 in.
(90 cm)
high

Normal
room
temperature

Indirect
sunlight

Ctenanthe is grown for its rosette of beautifully marked foliage rather than its insignificant white flowers. It is closely related to *Maranta* and *Calathea*, which are also grown for their leaves, but is more compact than either. A robust and bushy plant, it has leathery, lance-shaped leaves that grow to 18 in. (47 cm) in length and are dark green with silvery gray feathering above and wine-red to purple below. The form *Ctenanthe oppenheimiana* 'Tricolor' has leaves blotched with cream.

Caring for plants
Keep the potting soil moist during spring to autumn. In winter, apply only sufficient water to prevent the mix from drying out. Water with standard liquid fertilizer every 2 weeks in spring to autumn. Increase humidity by standing the pot on a tray of moist pebbles.

Making new plants
Detach the basal offsets from the rhizomatous roots as close to the parent plant as possible, or take tip cuttings of 3–4 leaves. Plant in standard potting soil; with cuttings, use hormone rooting preparation and base heat, if possible.

Ctenanthe oppenheimiana

Cyclamen persicum
Cyclamen

Various
heights

Cool,
55–65°F
(12–18°C)

Cool
light

Known as the "florist's cyclamen," these plants come in a variety of shapes and sizes. The nodding flowers can be ruffled, twisted, speckled, and sometimes scented, in shades of pure white to purple through a range of reds and pinks. The fleshy, dark green leaves can be large or tiny and usually have silver patterns. Seen more often at Christmastime, the cyclamen should last several weeks in flower—but do not buy from an outdoor vendor, because if the plant is chilled, the flowering period will be shortened.

Caring for plants
Keep the compost moist by watering from below because the tuber is only half-buried in the soil mix, and watering from above may cause it to rot. Water with standard liquid fertilizer every 2 weeks. Hygiene is critical to prevent gray mold, so as the flowers fade or the leaves die, remove immediately by twisting off as close as possible to the base.

Making new plants
Small plants can be raised from seed, but these cyclamen are usually bought as mature flowering plants.

Cyclamen persicum

Cymbidium spp.
Cymbidium

18 in.
(47 cm)
high

Normal
room
temperature

Indirect
sunlight

An epiphytic orchid, cymbidium is one of the easiest to begin with, especially the miniature hybrids. It has a rhizomatous root and stem system, with short pseudobulbs arising from it that carry the leathery, straplike leaves. The waxy flowers are borne on upright stalks, in shades of white, yellow, green, pink, red, or maroon. They open progressively along the flower stem over a period of several weeks in early summer, each bloom lasting up to 6 weeks. Each plant, once mature, produces up to 6 flowering stems per season.

Caring for plants
Keep the soil mix moist during spring to autumn. In winter, apply only sufficient water to prevent the medium from drying out. Increase the humidity by standing the pot on a tray of moist pebbles and misting regularly in high temperatures. Water with standard liquid fertilizer every 2 weeks in spring to summer. During the winter rest period, the temperature should be maintained at about 60°F (15°C).

Making new plants
Divide immediately after flowering by washing away the soil mix and cutting the rhizome with a clean, sharp knife. Each piece must have at least 2 pseudobulbs and some roots. Pot in a special orchid medium.

Cymbidium spp.

Cyperus involucratus
Umbrella grass

| 30 in. (75 cm) high | 24 in. (60 cm) spread | Normal room temperature | Indirect sunlight |

This is a clump-forming perennial with short basal leaves. It forms small, leafy bracts on the ends of tall, hollow green stems up to 30 in. (75 cm) long. In summer, it produces yellow flowers that turn brown after releasing their pollen, surrounded by up to 30 long bracts on top of long, 3-sided stems. The bracts are arranged spirally, like the spokes of an umbrella. It is an unusual foliage plant, ideal for adding height to a group display.

Caring for plants
Keep thoroughly moist at all times. This plant needs high humidity, so stand the container on a saucer of pebbles and keep the water level in the saucer high so it can evaporate around the leaves. Water with standard liquid fertilizer once a month during spring and early summer.

Making new plants
Divide mature plants in spring, and plant pieces in potting soil in individual pots.

Cyperus involucratus

Cyperus papyrus
Papyrus, Egyptian paper reed

10 ft. (3 m) or more high

Normal to warm room temperature, minimum 60°F (15°C)

Direct or indirect sunlight

Used for papermaking since ancient times, this is a large, clump-forming plant that needs plenty of space to grow to full size. It also needs a very moist environment and will thrive in boggy conditions, although it should not be completely submerged. The dark green "leaves" are actually bracts, borne at the top of tall, triangular stems, and above these are the flowers, which are carried in grasslike clusters.

Caring for plants
Overwatering this plant is almost impossible, but its high requirement for both water and humidity can be taken care of by standing the pot in a tray or saucer full of water. The plant can then take up as much water as it needs and the remains will increase the humidity. Water with standard liquid fertilizer once a month during spring to autumn. Dry air or drying out of the root-ball will result in brown tips on the bracts.

Making new plants
Divide mature plants in spring, and keep the potting soil moist.

Cyperus papyrus

Dahlia hybrida 'Dahlietta'
Pot dahlia

12 in.
(30 cm)
high

12 in.
(30 cm)
spread

Normal
room
temperature

Indirect
sunlight

This is a new collection of small forms of the popular garden dahlia, ideal for bringing color to the home, greenhouse, or porch. They are generally easy to grow, form neat, compact plants, and will flower profusely throughout much of the year. The lush foliage is mid-green or bronze, according to the variety, and the large, fully double flowers come in white and shades of pink, red, orange, and yellow. The Surprise series all have petals marked with secondary colors as flecks, splashes, brushstrokes, or picotee edging.

Caring for plants
Keep the soil mix moist at all times. Water with standard liquid fertilizer at half strength every 2 weeks while flowering. Pinching the very tip from 1 or 2 young shoots will encourage basal branching and build a stronger plant.

Making new plants
Take tip cuttings in spring and root at 68–74°F (20–23°C).

Top: *Dahlia hybrida* 'Dahlietta'—Surprise Purple Picotee;
Bottom: *Dahlia hybrida* 'Dahlietta'—Surprise Red Orange

Dendrobium spp.
Orchid

| 12–36 in. (30–90 cm) high | 10–12 in. (25–30 cm) spread | Normal room temperature | Indirect sunlight |

This is a group of evergreen or deciduous epiphytic orchids that are found naturally growing on other plants where they can use atmospheric moisture. Lance-shaped to oval leaves are produced from an elongated basal pseudobulb. The flowers are borne on single or multiple stems growing from nodes along the stems. These orchids resent disturbance and will flower best if the roots are slightly cramped. Depending on the variety, the beautiful, open flowers may be white, yellow, orange, pink, red, mauve, or purple, sometimes with different-colored central "lips."

Caring for plants
From spring to autumn, water and mist daily. Water with standard liquid fertilizer once a week. During the winter rest period, keep at about 60°F (15°C).

Making new plants
Divide when the mature plant fills the pot. Plant individual parts in fine-grade epiphytic orchid medium in a slatted basket to allow aerial roots to hang outside.

Dendrobium 'Emma Type'

Dianthus 'Dynasty'
Pink

15–20 in. (40–50 cm) high   Normal room temperature   Indirect sunlight

This impressive new series of F1 introductions (a Sweet William cross hybrid) is unusual in that it does not require a period of winter cold to promote flowering, so the plants will grow well and flower in a cool room, porch, or greenhouse. They will grow quickly to fill a container and will flower throughout the spring, summer, and autumn. Each has lightly scented, double flowers that resemble tiny carnations. They are well branched and upright, and the profuse flowers last well if they are cut for the vase. Flower colors include purple, red, white, and rose with a white picotee edging.

Caring for plants
Keep the potting soil moist at all times. Water with standard liquid fertilizer at half strength every 2 weeks. They can be planted in the garden after flowering because they are hardy, but they are not long-lived plants.

Making new plants
Plants have to be bought because seed seldom sets and does not grow true to type.

Dianthus 'Dynasty'

Dichondra argentea 'Silver Falls'
Kidneyweed

3 in. (7.5 cm) high. Up to 72 in. (180 cm) long   Normal room temperature   Direct or indirect sunlight

This is an amazingly tolerant plant that will thrive in a container, hanging basket, or indoor border, regardless of temperature. Its long silver-gray stems trail gracefully, giving a lacy effect and hiding any supporting structure or soil mix below. The shoots are self-branching, so pinching of the tips is not required, and they can reach 72 in. (180 cm) long. Each is covered with small, neatly fan-shaped silver leaves of around 1 in. (2.5 cm) in diameter, with a thick, supersoft texture. This vigorous, easy-to-grow plant is attractive on its own, but it will also mix with other colors to act as a foil.

Caring for plants
Keep the potting soil barely moist. Feed with standard liquid fertilizer at half strength every 2 weeks during spring and summer. Brighter light encourages more silvery foliage.

Making new plants
Sow seed in spring at 60°F (16°C). Transplant when 2 true leaves have expanded.

Top and bottom: Dichondra argentea 'Silver Falls'

Dieffenbachia maculata (syn. *D. picta*)
Dumb cane

Up to 60 in. (150 cm) high

Warm and humid, minimum 60°F (15°C)

Indirect sunlight. (Direct sunlight in winter)

Grown for their decorative foliage, dieffenbachias make striking feature plants either on their own or in a massed arrangement. The large, downward-pointing leaves are soft and fleshy, and marked with white or cream in varying amounts according to the cultivar. The thick, woody, unbranched stem is inclined to become bare at the base as the plant ages. *Dieffenbachia maculata* 'Tropic White' is a form with large, blotched white leaves; *D. maculata* 'Veerie' has green-yellow leaves with white blotches. The common name is derived from the effect of the poisonous sap on the mouth and tongue—it causes painful swelling—so wash your hands thoroughly after touching this plant.

Caring for plants
Keep the potting soil moist at all times. Water with standard liquid fertilizer every 2 weeks during spring to autumn.

Making new plants
Take tip cuttings 4–6 in. (10–15 cm) long in spring, dip in rooting hormone, and keep warm (70°F/20°C) in a plastic bag or heated propagator. Alternatively, take a 4 in. (10 cm) section of main stem with a growth bud and lay it horizontally on the potting soil and then treat it the same as a tip cutting.

Dieffenbachia maculata (syn. *D. picta*)

Dionaea muscipula
Venus flytrap

Up to
18 in.
(47 cm)
in flower

Warm and
humid

Direct sunlight
(except midday
in summer)

In its natural environment, this carnivorous
plant needs to supplement its nutrient intake
by trapping insects and digesting their contents,
and it has evolved a mechanism for catching
them that makes it a fascinating plant to watch.
It grows as a low rosette of leaves that have a
broadly winged, leafy petiole and 2 rounded,
hinged blades that become a glossy, bright red
in sunlight and are fringed with spines. When a
fly triggers the reaction, the leaves snap shut on
the prey. These plants are not normally very
long-lived in the home but are an interesting
addition while they last.

Caring for plants
Keep the soil thoroughly moist at all times.
Feed with extra flies or tiny pieces of meat
occasionally.

Making new plants
These are bought as small plants and cannot be
propagated in the home.

Dionaea muscipula

Dracaena cincta 'Tricolor'
Rainbow plant

60 in.
(150 cm)
high

Warm,
minimum
65°F (18°C)

Indirect
sunlight

Dracaenas are shrubby plants, often resembling palms with their arching leaves and bare, woody stems. They are grown for the color of their striking leaves, which are usually long and lance-shaped and striped or blotched with white, cream, and/or red. Because some mature dracaenas can grow to heights of 48 in. (120 cm) or more, they are ideal either within arrangements of other plants or as specimens in their own right. The common name of this plant comes from the dramatic leaf coloration, which is green, striped cream, and edged red. As the plant ages, the lower leaves turn down and fall, leaving the tuft of leaves atop a gradually lengthening, thin, bare stem. It will ultimately reach a height of about 60 in. (150 cm).

Caring for plants
Keep the soil mix thoroughly moist during spring to autumn. In winter, apply only sufficient water to prevent the mix from drying out. High humidity is important, so set the pot on a tray of moist pebbles. Water with standard liquid fertilizer every 2 weeks from spring to autumn.

Making new plants
Take tip cuttings 4–6 in. (10–15 cm) long from soft basal shoots in spring or early summer. Alternatively, longer pieces of mature woody stem can be inserted upright—the same way up as they were growing originally—into pots of a sterile medium to provide an instant "tree" effect; or 2 in. (5 cm) pieces of mature stem— each with at least one growth bud, a slight swelling under the bark—can be laid horizontally onto the medium, with the bud uppermost.

Dracaena cincta 'Tricolor'

Dracaena fragrans— Deremensis group

48 in.
(120 cm)
high

Warm,
minimum
65°F (18°C)

Indirect
sunlight

The plants in this group have long, arching, lance-shaped leaves overlapping one another all the way up and around the stem. They are slow-growing and ultimately reach 48 in. (120 cm) or more in height. *Dracaena fragrans* 'Lemon Lime' is a form with lime-green leaves that have pale yellow edges and a central stripe, *D. fragrans* 'Warneckei' features green leaves with 2 white stripes near the edge, and *D. fragrans* 'Yellow Stripe' has green leaves with rich yellow edges and a central stripe.

Caring for plants
Keep the soil mix thoroughly moist during spring to autumn. In winter, apply only sufficient water to prevent the mix from drying out. High humidity is important, so stand the pot on a tray of moist pebbles. Water with standard liquid fertilizer every 2 weeks from spring to autumn.

Making new plants
Take tip cuttings 4–6 in. (10–15 cm) long from soft basal shoots in spring or early summer. Alternatively, longer pieces of mature woody stem can be inserted upright—the same way they were growing originally—into pots of a sterile medium to provide an instant "tree" effect, or 2 in. (5 cm) pieces of mature stem— each with at least one growth bud, a slight swelling under the bark—can be laid horizontally onto the medium, with the bud uppermost.

Dracaena fragrans

Dracaena marginata 'Colorama'

60 in. (150 cm) high   Warm, minimum 65°F (18°C)   Indirect sunlight

There is a measure of confusion over the naming of the different plants within the *Dracaena* genus, and this plant bears a strong resemblance to *D. cincta* 'Tricolor'. The leaves are green, cream-striped, and broadly red-edged. As the plant ages, the lower leaves turn down and fall, leaving the tuft of leaves atop a gradually lengthening, thin, bare stem. It will ultimately reach a height of about 60 in. (150 cm). Dracaenas are shrubby plants, often resembling palms with their arching leaves and woody stems.

Caring for plants

Keep the soil mix thoroughly moist during spring to autumn. In winter, apply only sufficient water to prevent the compost from drying out. High humidity is important, so stand the pot on a tray of moist pebbles. Water with standard liquid fertilizer every 2 weeks from spring to autumn.

Making new plants

Take tip cuttings 4–6 in. (10–15 cm) long from soft basal shoots in spring or early summer. Alternatively, longer pieces of mature woody stem can be inserted upright—the same way they were growing originally—into pots of a sterile medium to provide an instant "tree" effect, or 2 in. (5 cm) pieces of mature stem—each with at least one growth bud, a slight swelling under the bark—can be laid horizontally onto the medium, with the bud uppermost.

Dracaena marginata 'Colorama'

Dracaena reflexa variegata
Song of India

48 in.
(120 cm)
high

Warm,
minimum
65°F (18°C)

Indirect
sunlight

This dracaena needs a warm location with high humidity to grow well. It is less woody and more graceful than most of its relatives and is beautifully marked with deep cream edges on the leaves. Like the other varieties, as the plant ages, the lower leaves turn down and fall, leaving the tuft of leaves on top of a gradually lengthening, thin, bare stem. This can be disguised by planting a screen of other houseplants around the base.

Caring for plants
Keep the soil mix thoroughly moist during spring to autumn. In winter, apply only sufficient water to prevent the mix from drying out. High humidity is important, so stand the pot on a tray of moist pebbles. Water with standard liquid fertilizer every 2 weeks from spring to autumn.

Making new plants
Take tip cuttings 4–6 in. (10–15 cm) long from soft basal shoots in spring or early summer. Alternatively, longer pieces of mature woody stem can be inserted upright—the same way they were growing originally—into pots of a sterile medium to provide an instant "tree" effect, or 2 in. (5 cm) pieces of mature stem—each with at least one growth bud, a slight swelling under the bark—can be laid horizontally onto the medium, with the bud uppermost.

Dracaena reflexa variegata

Dracaena sanderiana
Lucky bamboo, Ribbon plant

36 in. (90 cm) high	12 in. (30 cm) spread	Normal room temperature	Indirect sunlight

This plant has been around for a long time but has become popular recently when grown with twisted stems, giving it an architectural grace. It naturally forms a slender upright plant with canelike stems and long, graceful, rich green leaves with slightly wavy edges, which can be up to 8 in. (20 cm) long and taper to a point. It seldom flowers in cultivation. This particular plant is a favorite for interiors by devotees of feng shui, because it is reputed to enhance chi energy and bring good luck to both the giver and the recipient.

Caring for plants

If planted in potting soil, water freely from spring until autumn; then apply only enough water to prevent the mix from drying out and water with standard liquid fertilizer once a month during spring and early summer. Lucky bamboo is also often grown in water. In this case, simply change the water at least every other week to keep it fresh.

Making new plants

Take semiripe cuttings of stem sections in summer, and root in a sterile medium, or stand in fresh water.

Top and Bottom: *Dracaena sanderiana*

Echeveria agavoides
Echeveria

6 in.
(15 cm)
high

Normal
room
temperature

Direct
sunlight

Fleshy, triangular mid-green leaves are arranged in a rosette around the short stem. They are sharply pointed and waxy, with transparent margins. The flower head is double-branched, with small flowers that open successively from the base of the curled spike toward the tip. Each is bell-shaped, pink-orange outside, yellow within, and about ½ in. (12 mm) across. If the plant is grown in full sunlight, the edges of the leaves will take on a reddish tint. *Echeveria agavoides* 'Metallica' has purple-lilac leaves, turning olive bronze.

Caring for plants
Keep the soil mix barely moist at all times. Overwatering to even a small extent will cause soft growth that is liable to rot. Water with standard liquid fertilizer once a month during spring to autumn. Keep the plant at a winter temperature of 55–60°F (12–15°C) for the winter rest.

Making new plants
Take leaf cuttings or remove offsets, and root in a sterile medium.

Echeveria agavoides

Echeveria secunda
Echeveria

| 12 in. (30 cm) high | Normal room temperature | Direct sunlight |

This is a plant with short stems that forms clumps as it produces offsets. The rounded, succulent leaves are tipped with a bristle and feel waxy to the touch. They are up to 2 in. (5 cm) long and pale green in color, tipped and edged with red. Red flowers with a yellow center may be produced in early summer on stems up to 12 in. (30 cm) long. *Echeveria secunda* var. *glauca* is a form with gray-blue leaves.

Caring for plants
Keep the soil mix barely moist at all times; overwatering to even a small extent will cause soft growth that is liable to rot. Water with standard liquid fertilizer once a month during spring to autumn. Keep the plant at a winter temperature of 55–60°F (12–15°C) for the winter rest period.

Making new plants
Take leaf cuttings or remove offsets, and plant the soil mix.

Top: *Echeveria secunda* f. *monstrosa*; Bottom: *Echeveria secunda* f. *cristata*

Echinocactus texensis
Barrel cactus

| 5–8 in.
(12.5–20 cm)
high | 12 in.
(30 cm)
spread | Normal to
warm room
temperature
spring–autumn | Direct
sunlight |

In the wild, the echinocactus can live for more than 100 years, eventually forming a mound of perhaps 36 in. (90 cm) across. The shape is that of a slightly flattened ball, with between 13 and 27 ribs. Each areole produces a cluster of red-brown spines, with one central spine of up to 3 in. (7.5 cm) in length, directed downward and strongly curved. The flowers are 2 in. (5 cm) across, pink to orange-red in the throat, with paler margins.

Caring for plants
Keep the soil mix moist from spring to autumn, but during winter apply only sufficient water to prevent the mix from drying out. Water with standard liquid tomato fertilizer once a month in spring and summer. During the winter rest period, keep at 50°F (10°C), but no lower than 40°F (5°C).

Making new plants
Sow seed in special cactus medium and keep moist but not wet. Transplant or repot mature plants in spring.

Echinocactus texensis

Elatostema repens var. *pulchrum*
Rainbow vine, Satin pellionia

Stems to 18 in. (47 cm) high	Normal room temperature all year. Minimum 55°F (12°C)	Indirect sunlight

A low, spreading plant, grown for its fleshy, purple-tinted stems and striking leaves that are ¾–2 in. (2–5 cm) long. They are emerald green in color, marked with a dull black-green along the midrib and veins above and light purple below. This is a useful plant in a terrarium or bottle garden while it is small, or placed at the front of an arrangement to disguise the container and soften the outline, or in a hanging basket. As it grows, it will form roots wherever the stems are in contact with the potting soil.

Caring for plants
Keep the soil mix thoroughly moist during spring to autumn. In winter, apply only sufficient water to prevent the mix from drying out. Water with standard liquid fertilizer once a month in spring to summer. Mist occasionally in high temperatures, shelter from drafts, and do not allow direct sunlight to scorch the leaves.

Making new plants
Take tip cuttings in spring or summer, and root in a sterile medium. Lift layers at any time.

Elatostema repens var. *pulchrum*

Epiphyllum crenatum
Orchid cactus

36 in.
(90 cm)
high

36 in.
(90 cm)
spread

Normal to
cool room
temperature

Indirect
sunlight

This vigorous, bushy, semiepiphytic cactus has an upright habit with a cylindrical main stem and leaflike, gray-green branches. These have a wavy, toothed edging and are up to 5 in. (12.5 cm) wide. The striking, fragrant, funnel-shaped flowers are creamy white, with green, pink, or pale yellow outer segments, and may be up to 8 in. (20 cm) long. They are produced in summer and last for 2 to 3 days but are diurnal—they open during the day and close again at night.

Care of plants
Water freely from spring until autumn; then apply only enough water to prevent the medium from drying out. This cactus likes high humidity, so mist regularly or stand the pot on a saucer of pebbles and keep the water level high enough to evaporate around the foliage. Water with standard liquid tomato fertilizer at half strength every 2 weeks from spring to late summer.

Making new plants
Take stem cuttings in spring, and root in a sterile medium.

Epiphyllum crenatum

Epipremnum aureum
Devil's ivy, Golden pothos

60 in.
(150 cm)
or more
high

Warm,
minimum
65°F (18°C)

Indirect
sunlight

The angular stems of this woody vine can be grown to either climb up a moist moss pole or cascade down from a high planter or hanging basket. They are striped with yellow or white and have aerial roots. The heart-shaped leaves are large, between 6–12 in. (15–30 cm) long, and are green striped with yellow or white. *Epipremnum aureum* 'Marble Queen' has a white leaf stalk, green leaves streaked white and moss green, and white stems streaked with green. *E. aureum* 'Tricolor' has leaves boldly variegated in white and off-white stems and leafstalks.

Caring for plants
Keep the soil mix moist during spring to autumn. In winter, apply only sufficient water to prevent the mix from drying out. Water with standard liquid fertilizer every 2 weeks in spring to summer. To maintain high humidity, place the pot on a tray of moist pebbles. Overwatering will cause root rot, and drafts will cause damage to the foliage. Too little light will cause the leaf colors to revert to green.

Making new plants
Take tip cuttings 4 in. (10 cm) long in spring or early summer, and root in a sterile starting medium.

Epipremnum aureum

Euphorbia pulcherrima
Poinsettia

12–18 in.
(30–47 cm)
high

Normal
room
temperature

Indirect
sunlight

The poinsettia has become an essential element of decoration at Christmastime, with its cheerful, brightly colored flower heads. The long-lasting scarlet, pink, or cream "flowers" are actually large bracts surrounding the true flowers, which are tiny, yellow, and short-lived. It is normal to discard the plant once the bracts fade, but it is possible to keep it for the green foliage. Bringing it back into color for a subsequent year is not easy. When purchasing a poinsettia, look for small, unopened flower buds in the center of the bracts and be sure that it has been kept indoors—never buy one that has been standing outside.

Caring for plants
Water thoroughly, but allow the mix to dry slightly before watering again. Fertilizing is not necessary unless the plant is to be kept after the bracts fade.

Making new plants
Take tip cuttings 3 in. (7.5 cm) long when growth starts in spring. Note that the plant exudes an irritant milky latex from cut surfaces, so be sure to seal the cuttings by placing them in water.

Euphorbia pulcherrima

Eustoma grandiflorum
Prairie gentian

24 in.
(60 cm)
high

Cool room
temperature

Indirect
sunlight

An upright annual or biennial, eustoma is grown for its attractive flowers and foliage that last well when cut. The pointed oval, thinly fleshy leaves are 3 in. (7.5 cm) long, gray-green, and thickly covered with a bloom that can be rubbed off with the finger and thumb. The bell-shaped flowers are borne in summer on 2 in. (5 cm) stalks, either singly or in clusters. Each is satiny, 2 in. (5 cm) across, and is white, blue, pink, or purple, with a darker central patch; the short tube is paler than the lobes. In mild areas, eustoma can be grown outdoors, but where the weather isn't consistent, they will thrive in a cool greenhouse. The stems are not very strong, and the plant will need support.

Caring for plants
Keep the soil mix moist from spring to autumn. In winter, apply only sufficient water to prevent the plants from drying out. Water with standard liquid fertilizer every 2 weeks during spring to autumn.

Making new plants
Sow seed in autumn or late winter in a seed-starting medium.

Eustoma grandiflorum

Exacum affine
Persian violet, German violet

12 in.
(30 cm)
high

Normal room
temperature,
but avoid
drafts

Indirect
sunlight

This is a short-lived perennial plant, generally treated as an annual and discarded after flowering. It has glossy green leaves and an abundance of fragrant sky blue to pale violet or rich purple flowers with prominent golden stamens. If the plant is in bud when bought, it will flower throughout summer and autumn.

Caring for plants

Keep the soil thoroughly moist. Exacums like high humidity, so stand the pot on a tray of moist pebbles. Water with standard liquid fertilizer every 2 weeks while the plant is in flower. Pick off fading flowers to extend the flowering period.

Making new plants

Sow seed in late summer for the following year or in spring for a slightly later flowering in the same year.

Exacum affine

Fargesia nitida (syn. *Arundinaria*)
Fountain bamboo

15 ft.
(5 m) high

Tolerant of a
wide range of
temperatures

Indirect
sunlight

This is a pretty, slow-growing bamboo originating from China. It will gradually form a dense thicket of purple-green canes, each marked with powdery white under the leaf nodes. The canes do not branch until they are in their second year of growth, when the upper part of the stems produces a cluster of purple branchlets. Narrow, tapering mid-green leaves are produced in abundance on all stems.

Caring for plants
Keep the soil mix moist at all times. Water with standard liquid fertilizer once a month during spring to autumn. This is a hardy bamboo in all but the coldest areas, so it can be planted outdoors once it has outgrown its position indoors.

Making new plants
Divide clumps of a mature plant, or take cuttings of rhizomes in spring. Root in a sterile medium in individual pots.

Fargesia nitida (syn. *Arundinaria*)

x *Fatshedera lizei*
Ivy tree

48 in. (120 cm) high

Variegated forms above 60°F (15°C)

Cool light, variegated forms need more light than green ones

The result of a breeding cross between two distinct genera within the same plant family is denoted by the x before the name. In this case, the result, x *Fatshedera,* is an attractive evergreen plant bearing characteristics of both parents, and the general ease of cultivation of both. From *Fatsia* come the wide-spreading glossy leaves, from *Hedera* the sprawling stems, which can easily be trained up canes or pinched to produce a more bushy effect. The young leaves are covered in rust-colored hairs. x *F. lizei* 'Pia' has wavy green leaves, x *F. lizei* 'Annemieke' has leaves marked with yellow, and x *F. lizei* 'Variegata' has leaves with white markings.

Caring for plants
Keep the soil mix moist from spring to autumn, but apply only sufficient water in winter to prevent it from drying out. In warmer locations, increase humidity by standing the pot on a tray of moist pebbles. Water with standard liquid fertilizer every 2 weeks during spring to summer. Keep variegated forms above 60°F (15°C) at all times, but green forms will tolerate a much cooler location, even a cool greenhouse.

Making new plants
Take tip cuttings 4 in. (10 cm) long, or stem cuttings 2 in. (5 cm) long, in spring to summer. Dip in rooting hormone and enclose in a plastic bag. Place in a warm, bright location.

x *Fatshedera lizei*

Fatsia japonica
Japanese fatsia

| 60 in. (150 cm) high in 2–3 years | Preferably cool, below 60°F (15°C) in summer and below 45°F (7°C) in winter | Cool light |

This is a wide-spreading evergreen shrub that can be grown indoors or out. It has large, leathery, many-fingered leaves that leave prominent scars on the woody stem as they fall. Fatsia makes an impressive specimen plant, but it grows quickly and needs plenty of room. The foliage tends to be a lighter color indoors than outdoors, and the creamy white flowers will be produced only on a mature plant that is kept in cool conditions.

Caring for plants

Keep the soil mix thoroughly moist from spring to autumn, but just moist in winter. Water with standard liquid fertilizer every 2 weeks during spring to autumn. Large plants can be pruned hard in spring to remove up to half the growth.

Making new plants

Take stem cuttings 2 in. (5 cm) long during spring to summer, remove the lower leaves, and dip the end in rooting hormone. Enclose in a plastic bag or propagation case at around 60°F (15°C) in a well-lit position.

Fatsia japonica

Ficus benjamina
Weeping fig

72 in.
(180 cm)
high

Normal room
temperature
(away from
drafts)

Indirect
sunlight

This is a graceful tree, which will grow to 72 in. (180 cm) or more and make a beautiful specimen tree or form a centerpiece for a mixed planting. The branches droop downward as they grow, dripping with shiny, thin leathery leaves, which change from mid- to dark green as the plant ages. The little figs are borne in pairs, and if they are pollinated, they mature to orange-red, scarlet, and finally purplish black. The *Ficus,* or Fig, genus encompasses some 800 species of trees, shrubs, and woody root-climbing or strangling vines. They originate in tropical and subtropical areas and make good indoor plants because they are not particularly demanding. The leaves are usually entire—one whole shape, with no lobes or teeth—and the tiny flowers are borne within a fleshy, hollow receptacle (a syconium or fig), with a minute hole that insects crawl into, pollinating the flower.

Caring for plants
Keep thoroughly moist at all times, but not wet. Apply standard liquid fertilizer once a month in spring through autumn.

Making new plants
Take tip cuttings 4 in. (10 cm) long in spring. The cutting will root better if the bottom ½ in. (12 mm) has become light brown and woody. To prevent the latex from forming a cap on the base of the cutting, strip the leaves from the lower third and place in water for 30 minutes. Remove, shake off the water, and dip the cut surface only in rooting hormone, then insert into compost and seal into a plastic bag in a bright place, out of direct sun.

Ficus benjamina

Ficus binnendykii
(was *F. longifolia*)
Narrow-leaf fig

| 60 in. (150 cm) high | Normal room temperature | Indirect sunlight |

This fig grows into an attractive, glossy shrub or small tree, making it both an attractive feature plant or an ideal foil in a mixed arrangement. It has graceful, drooping, pointed-tipped foliage that changes size and shape as the plant ages from long and lance-shaped at around 8 x 4 in. (20 x 10 cm) when it is young to a more oblong 3½ x 1½ in. (8 x 4 cm) in a mature specimen. The egg-shaped figs are borne singly or in pairs, and are 4 in. (10 cm) across. The *Ficus*, or Fig, genus originates in tropical and subtropical areas, and they make good indoor plants because they are easy to look after. The leaves are usually entire and they have tiny flowers that are borne within a fleshy, hollow receptacle—a syconium or fig.

Caring for plants
Keep thoroughly moist at all times, but not wet. Apply standard liquid fertilizer once a month spring through autumn.

Making new plants
In spring, take tip cuttings 4 in. (10 cm) long, which will root better if the bottom ½ in. (12 mm) has become light brown and woody. To prevent the latex from forming a cap on the base of the cutting, strip the leaves from the lower third and place in water for 30 minutes. Remove, shake off the water, and dip only the cut surface in rooting hormone; insert into a sterile medium and seal into a plastic bag in a bright place, out of direct sun.

Ficus binnendykii

Ficus deltoidea
Mistletoe fig

36 in.
(90 cm)
high

Normal room
temperature
(away from
drafts)

Indirect
sunlight

Known also as *Ficus deltoidea* var. *diversifolia*, this is a twiggy shrub with small rounded-triangular leaves that are bright green on the top surface and olive brown beneath. From a young age, it regularly produces pairs of round, pea-size, dull-yellow inedible fruit in the leaf axils. The *Ficus*, or Fig, genus encompasses some 800 species of trees—many of which contain a milky latex—shrubs, and woody root-climbing or strangling vines. They originate in tropical and subtropical areas and make good indoor plants because they are not particularly demanding.

Caring for plants
Keep moist at all times, but not wet. Apply standard liquid fertilizer once a month in spring through autumn.

Making new plants
Take 4 in. (10 cm) long tip cuttings in spring. The cutting will root better if the bottom ½ in. (12 mm) is light brown and woody. To prevent the latex from forming a cap on the base of the cutting, strip the leaves from the lower third and place in water for 30 minutes. Remove, shake off the water, and dip only the cut surface in rooting hormone; then insert into a sterile medium and seal into a plastic bag in a bright place, out of direct sun.

Ficus deltoidea

Ficus elastica
Rubber plant

78 in.
(195 cm)
high

Normal room
temperature
(away from
drafts)

Indirect
sunlight

This is the original rubber plant that has
been popular as an indoor plant for many
years, although it has been largely superseded
by a number of newer cultivars with a more
compact habit or colored leaf markings. The
glossy leaves are large and leathery, with a
prominent midrib and a pointed tip. They arise
from a single tall stem, which rarely produces
side shoots unless the top is removed. *Ficus
elastica* 'Robusta' has rather larger and wider
leaves, in *F. elastica* 'Decora' the leaves are
broad and shiny with a white midrib, *F. elastica*
'Tricolor' has gray-green leaves that are variegated
pink and cream, and *F. elastica* 'Variegata' has
pale green leaves with a white or yellow margin.

Caring for plants
Keep thoroughly moist at all times, but not wet.
Apply standard liquid fertilizer once a month in
spring through autumn.

Making new plants
Take tip cuttings 4 in. (10 cm) long in spring.
The cutting will root better if the bottom ½ in.
(12 mm) has become light brown and woody.
To prevent the latex from forming a cap on the
base of the cutting, strip the leaves from the
lower third and place in water for 30 minutes.
Remove, shake off the water, and dip only the
cut surface in rooting hormone; then insert into
a sterile medium and seal into a plastic bag in a
bright place, out of direct sun.

Ficus elastica

Ficus lyrata
Fiddle-leaf or banjo fig

10 ft. (3 m) high	7–10 ft. (2–3 m) spread	Normal room temperature	Indirect light

This evergreen plant from West and Central Africa has a treelike habit. The dark, glossy green leaves have a leathery texture and are up to 18 in. (47 cm) in length and fiddle-shaped. Small, spherical fruits up to 2 in. (5 cm) in diameter are produced singly or in pairs on mature plants, if conditions allow. These fruits are dark green, becoming green with white markings when they ripen. This is a wonderful foliage plant for the entrance hallway or garden room, where the dramatic foliage can be fully appreciated.

Caring for plants
Water freely from spring until autumn; then apply only enough water to prevent the soil mix from drying out. Water with standard liquid fertilizer once a month during spring and early summer. Prune in late winter or early spring, if required.

Making new plants
Take semiripe cuttings in spring or summer, and root in a sterile medium.

Top and Bottom: *Ficus lyrata*

Ficus pumila
Creeping fig

Up to 24 in. (60 cm) high—named varieties are smaller

Normal to warm room temperature

Partial shade

This plant is a complete contrast to the taller, treelike figs because it is a low-growing, small-leaved trailer or climber. It has small, slightly puckered green leaves and an abundance of aerial roots that will root easily into a moist surface such as a moss pole, although the plant is equally attractive as a trailing plant or as groundcover. *Ficus pumila* 'Minima' is very small and slender, slow-growing, *F. pumila* 'Sonny' has very small leaves with cream edges, and *F. pumila* 'Variegata' is a form with vigorous leaves marbled with white or cream.

Caring for plants
Keep the soil mix just moist at all times. Water with standard liquid fertilizer every 2 weeks during spring to summer. Sponge the leaves clean at intervals to remove dust, taking care not to damage young foliage because any marks will not disappear. Wounds to most figs result in the oozing of milky latex, often in large quantities. This can be stemmed by applying powdered charcoal, cotton wool, or a small piece of paper towel to the wound to help the latex coagulate.

Making new plants
Take tip cuttings up to 4 in. (10 cm) long in spring through summer. Roots will form easily, even in water. Pot several rooted cuttings together to give an instant bushy effect.

Ficus pumila

Fittonia verschaffeltii var. *argyroneura*
Mosaic plant

6 in.
(15 cm)
high

Preferably
a constant
65°F (18°C)

Partial
shade

Fittonias are creeping, stem-rooting evergreen plants that grow naturally in the warm, moist conditions of the tropical rain forests. The downy leaves are 2½–4 in. (6–10 cm) long, oval-shaped, and a deep olive-green with a dense network of colored veins, carried on stems of 3½ in. (8 cm). The flowers are white, in slender 4-angled spikes up to 3½ in. (8 cm) long, but they are largely concealed by bracts. The *Verschaffeltii* group are attractive small plants with rose-pink veins, so that the whole leaf is pink flushed. *Fittonia verschaffeltii argyroneura* group, known as the silver net plant, has slightly larger leaves that are emerald green, closely net veined with silver white.

Caring for plants
Careful watering is essential: Too much, and the roots will rot; too little, and the leaves will shrivel and drop off. Keep barely moist at all times. Water with half-strength liquid fertilizer every 2 weeks from spring to summer.

Making new plants
Take 2-in. (5-cm)-long tip cuttings in spring or layer the plant by placing the pot inside a larger one filled with potting soil. Pin the tip of a shoot down onto the soil mix with a wire hoop until it roots; then gently sever it from the parent and transplant it.

Fittonia verschaffeltii var. argyroneura

Freesia spp.
Freesia

Up to 18 in.
(47 cm)
high

Normal
room
temperature

Indirect
sunlight, some
direct
sunlight

Normally found as cut flowers in the florist's shop, freesias are easy to grow from dry corms and provide a long-lasting display. The funnel-shaped flowers are highly fragrant and are held on arching stems in a range of colors, including red, orange, pink, white, blue, lilac, and yellow. The leaves are long, thin, and lance-shaped, bright green, and arranged in a flat, fan shape.

Caring for plants
Keep the soil mix moist until flowering has finished; then gradually reduce to dry the corms and get them ready for winter storage. Water with standard liquid fertilizer every week once the flower buds appear.

Making new plants
Corms do not flower a second time—new corms develop from lateral buds. These can be carefully detached and transplanted.

Freesia

Fuchsia spp.
Ladies' eardrops

Various
heights

Normal room
temperature

Indirect
sunlight

Fuchsias are most commonly associated with outdoor plantings, but many of the small varieties make attractive and colorful plants for indoors or the greenhouse. They will brighten any display with their intricate, long-lasting blooms. Most are prolific flowerers, with lush green, bronze, or variegated foliage. Flower forms may be single, semidouble, or fully double, and colors range from white through shades of pink and red to deepest magenta and purple. *Fuschia* 'Ballet Girl' only grows 12–18 in. (30–47 cm) high and produces large double flowers of cerise and white. Trailing forms such as 'Marinka' are ideal for displaying on a pedestal and will reach 12 in. (30 cm) high with a spread of up to 24 in. (60 cm). Choose a smaller-growing variety for indoors.

Caring for plants
Keep the soil mix moist at all times. Water with standard liquid tomato fertilizer at half strength once a week from spring to autumn.

Making new plants
Take softwood cuttings in spring or semiripe cuttings in late summer, and root in a sterile medium.

Fuchsia

Gardenia augusta (was *G. jasminoides*)
Gardenia

| 18 in. (47 cm) high | Normal room temperature | Indirect sunlight |

This is a bushy, evergreen, acid-loving shrub, grown for its waxy flowers, which are up to 3 in. (7.5 cm) across, white, and intensely fragrant. They are usually double—many-petaled—but also occur as 2 layers of petals. The lance-shaped, dark green leaves are 2–4 in. (5–10 cm) long, glossy, and leathery. *Gardenia augusta* 'Radicans Variegata' is a miniature form that grows into a mound shape and has small white flowers and leaves that are glossy, tinted gray, and edged in white. *G. augusta* 'Veitchiana' is a more upright and compact form, with small, pure white, fully double, and very fragrant flowers and small, bright green leaves.

Caring for plants
While flower buds are forming, a constant, draft-free 62–63°F (17°C) is needed to prevent bud loss. Otherwise, normal room temperature is fine. Keep the soil mix moist during spring to autumn, using soft water or rainwater. High humidity is essential while the flower buds are forming, so stand the pot on a tray of moist pebbles, and mist frequently. In winter, apply only sufficient water to prevent the mix from drying out. Fertilize with acid fertilizer every 2 weeks from spring to autumn. Any pruning should be done immediately after flowering; cut to an outward-facing bud.

Making new plants
Take 3-in. (7.5-cm)-long tip cuttings in spring, dip in rooting hormone, and push into pots of an ericaceous soil mix. Cover and give bottom heat, if possible, in a bright position out of direct sun.

Gardenia augusta

Gerbera jamesonii
Transvaal daisy, Barberton daisy

12–24 in.
(30–60 cm)
high,
depending
on variety

Normal
room
temperature

Indirect
sunlight. Some
direct sunlight,
but not midday
in summer

There are a wide range of seed selections of this popular flowering pot plant, bringing a range of different heights and flower colors from red to orange, yellow, pink, and white, in single or double forms. The taller strains need staking to support the weight of the flower head. The flowers appear from May to August, from rosettes of hairy, lobed, mid-green leaves. Single flower varieties include California Mixed, which is tall and multicolored, and Parade Mixed, which is shorter, with early, long-lasting flowers. Double-flower varieties are Festival Mixture Pandora series, which is early flowering; Sunburst Mixture with large flowers to 4 in. (10 cm) across; Happipot Mixture with dark green leaves; and Fantasia Double Strain, which has flowers to 5 in. (12.5 cm) across with a quilled center.

Caring for plants
Keep the soil mix moist at all times and water with standard liquid fertilizer every 2 weeks. Discard the plant after flowering.

Making new plants
Sow seed in a seed-starting medium.

Gerbera jamesonii

Gloriosa superba 'Rothschildiana'
Glory lily

| 48 in. (120 cm) high | Average room temperature | Indirect sunlight. Some direct sunlight, but not at midday in summer |

This is a tuberous perennial plant, which climbs by means of tendrils at the tips of the leaves. Each tuber produces between 1 and 4 stems of 48 in. (120 cm) or more in length, but they are weak and must be supported. The flowers are produced in midsummer and have strongly swept-back petals of scarlet or ruby red with a yellow base.

Caring for plants
Keep the soil mix thoroughly moist from spring to autumn. As the flower buds begin to swell, keep the plant warm and well watered and mist in high temperatures. Water with standard liquid fertilizer every 2 weeks during spring to summer. Store the tuber over the winter in the pot in a frost-free position and keep the soil mix barely moist.

Making new plants
Plant new tubers upright in a pot, with the tip 1 in. (2.5 cm) below the surface. As the plant matures, offsets can be severed at repotting time in spring and potted separately.

Gloriosa superba 'Rothschildiana'

Grevillea robusta
Silky oak

72–84 in. (180–210 cm) high

Tolerant of a wide range of temperatures, winter minimum 65°F (18°C)

Direct sunlight, except at midday in summer

With its graceful, 12-in. (30-cm)-long, arching foliage, this plant is an ideal mixer for a large arrangement. The leaves are bronze to dark green, ferny, and covered on the underside with silky hairs. It grows quickly, reaching 12 in. (30 cm) in its first year, which makes a young plant a good subject for a table-top arrangement, and up to 72–84 in. (180–210 cm) in 4–5 years, making it more useful in a large porch or greenhouse. The leaves tend to lose their ferny appearance as the plant ages, and it may be preferable to start again with a young plant after 3–4 years.

Caring for plants

Keep the soil mix moist from spring to autumn, but barely moist in winter. Water with standard liquid fertilizer every 2 weeks during spring to summer.

Making new plants

Sow seed in an ericaceous soil mix in spring or summer. Position in a bright spot, out of direct sun, at a temperature of 55–60°F (12–15°C).

Top and Bottom: *Grevillea robusta*

Guzmania lingulata

Guzmania lingulata
Scarlet star

12 in.
(30 cm)
high

Up to
24 in.
(60 cm)
spread

Warm
(above
65°F/18°C)

Indirect
sunlight

Although the arching, 18 in. (47 cm) leaves of *Guzmania lingulata* are an attractive, rich dark brown at the base, fading to green, and sometimes striped with violet, the plant is usually grown for its flowers. More accurately, because the flowers themselves are small and yellow, the attraction is the bracts that surround the flower and form a bright crimson star-shaped cup at the top of a 12 in. (30 cm) stalk.

Caring for plants
Keep the soil mix thoroughly moist at all times, and also add a little water to the central cup. High humidity is essential, so keep the plant on a tray of damp pebbles and mist the foliage every day. Water with half-strength liquid fertilizer once a month on the soil surface, the leaves, and into the cup.

Making new plants
With a sharp knife, take 3–4 in. (7.5–10 cm) offsets in spring, and root in a sterile medium. Rooting should take 3–4 months.

Hatiora gaertneri
(was *Rhipsalidopsis*)
Easter cactus

30–40 cm
(12–15 in.)
high

Normal
room
temperature
at all times

Indirect
sunlight

The flowers of *Hatiora gaertneri* are an intense red color and are produced either singly or in groups of 2 or 3, over a period of several weeks in spring—although each individual flower may only last 2 or 3 days. They arise from a cluster of long brown bristles at the end of new stem segments. The segments themselves are thin, flattened, and up to 1¼ in. (3 cm) long, forming stems that are upright at first, then droop down as they get longer, making this an ideal plant for a hanging basket.

Caring for plants

Apart from a 3–4 week rest period after flowering, when the soil mix should only be given enough water to prevent it from drying out, keep the mix moist at all times. Water with standard liquid tomato fertilizer every 2 weeks in spring, from the appearance of the flower buds until the last bud has opened. Stop fertilizing during the rest period; then apply standard liquid fertilizer once a month during the rest of the year. Repot after the rest period in spring.

Making new plants

Take at least 2 segments by breaking them carefully from the parent plant. Push deeply enough into a small pot of potting soil to stand upright; then water gently to settle the mix. Several cuttings can be inserted into a larger pot for an immediate effect.

Hatiora gaertneri

Haworthia margaritifera

Haworthia margaritifera
Pearl haworthia

4–7 in.
(10–18 cm)
high

Cool

Indirect
sunlight

This is an unusual clump-forming, stemless plant with a rosette of around 50 tightly packed, incurved to upright, fat, rigid, dark or purple-green leaves with sharp red-brown tips, covered in rough, pearly white warty lumps. Branched stems up to 15 in. (40 cm) long form in summer, bearing tube-shaped brown to yellow-green flowers in clusters of up to 6 in. (15 cm) long. These are best grown as for cacti, in individual pots, or in groups together in a larger container.

Caring for plants
Keep the medium moist from spring to autumn. In winter, apply only sufficient water to prevent the plant from drying out. Do not allow the soil mix to become wet at any time, or the roots will rot. Water with low-nitrogen liquid fertilizer once a month during spring to autumn.

Making new plants
Sow seed, take offsets, or divide the mature plant in spring. Plant in a fast-draining soil mix.

Hedera canariensis
Algerian ivy, Canary Island ivy

84 in. (210 cm) or more high

Tolerant of a wide range of temperatures

Indirect sunlight

A vigorous, large-leaved ivy that thrives in cooler locations indoors, this is equally useful for climbing, trailing, weaving around posts or banisters, or as a groundcover in a planted area or large container. The stems and undersides of young leaves are covered with small red hairs, and until the plant reaches its adult phase—when the leaves change shape and texture—they are lobed, thick, matte, and leathery. *Hedera canariensis* 'Gloire de Marengo' has leaves that are light green, edged and splashed with creamy white.

Caring for plants

Keep the soil mix moist during spring to autumn. In winter, apply only sufficient water to prevent drying out. In high temperatures, increase the humidity by misting or standing the pot on a tray of moist pebbles. Water with standard liquid fertilizer every 2 weeks from spring to autumn. Variegated plants will lose their leaf markings if they are placed in too dark a location.

Making new plants

Adventitious roots are produced at leaf nodes along each stem, so propagation can be done by layering or by taking tip cuttings and rooting in water or potting soil.

Hedera canariensis

Hedera helix
English ivy

36 in. (90 cm) high

Tolerant of a wide range of temperatures

Indirect sunlight

The best-known of all the ivies, with a distinctive shape to the leaves, this is a bushy, densely leaved plant, ideal for trailing and groundcover. Within the grouping, there are a wide range of variations in coloring and leaf shape, although all are 3–5 lobed. The stems are stiff, but only self-supporting where the aerial roots can grip. They branch regularly, so the foliage fans out as it grows, and it can be used to trail from a shelf or from the front of a container to disguise it.

Caring for plants

Keep moist from spring to autumn, but apply only sufficient water to prevent it from drying out in winter. In high temperatures, increase the humidity by misting or standing the pot on a tray of moist pebbles. Water with standard liquid fertilizer every 2 weeks from spring to autumn. Variegated plants will lose their leaf markings if they are placed in too dark a location.

Making new plants

Since adventitious roots are produced at leaf nodes along each stem, propagation can be done by layering. Otherwise, take tip cuttings and root in water or potting soil.

Hedera helix

Helianthus 'Ballad'
Sunflower

20–24 in.
(50–60 cm)
high

12 in.
(30 cm)
spread

Normal
room
temperature

Direct
sunlight

This is a dwarf F1 hybrid of the traditional sunflower that remains compact, making it ideal for use in containers indoors. One of its main attractions is that it does not produce pollen, so it can be perfect for the hay-fever sufferer. The lush foliage is a glossy green and is much more resistant to mildew than other sunflowers. The cheerful flowers have bright golden yellow petals with a dark center and will be larger if the plant is grown in full sunlight. It will also have a stronger stem and set more secondary buds in a well-lit location.

Caring for plants

Keep thoroughly moist, but not wet, and fertilize with a standard liquid fertilizer every 2 weeks during spring and summer.

Making new plants

Sow seed at 68–72°F (20–22°C) and cover; it will take 4 days for germination. Within 10–12 weeks from sowing, the new plants should be flowering.

Top and bottom: Helianthus 'Ballad'

Hibiscus moscheutos
Mallow

24–36 in.
(60–90 cm)
high

24 in.
(60 cm)
spread

Normal to
cool room
temperature

Direct or
indirect
sunlight

New forms of hibiscus, particularly the Luna series, produce some truly enormous blooms during the summer months. They can be up to 5 in. (12.5 cm) in diameter and occur in shades of red and creamy yellow. They grow reasonably tall, up to 36 in. (90 cm), making them ideal for the hall, porch, or greenhouse, where they can be appreciated without getting in the way. They are tolerant of both cool and hot temperatures, although like many plants, they dislike midday summer sun if they are behind glass. They also do not mind a drought, although they do not like being overwatered. *Hibiscus moscheutos* 'Luna Blush' has white petals with a pale pink rim and a dark red eye.

Caring for plants
Keep the soil mix moist, but allow to dry slightly between waterings. Water with standard liquid fertilizer every 2 weeks during spring and summer. This plant prefers slightly acid potting soil.

Making new plants
Take softwood cuttings in spring and root in a slightly acid soilless medium.

Hibiscus moscheutos

Hibiscus rosa-sinensis
Chinese hibiscus, Rose of China

72–84 in.
(180–210
cm)
high

Normal room
temperature.
Winter
minimum 55°F
(12°C)

Direct
sunlight,
except
midday
in summer

Hibiscus is one of the few flowering plants that really enjoys a sunny windowsill. It is a long-lived shrub, even indoors, and with care will last up to 20 years. The leaves are large and glossy, but the main attraction is the profusion of 4–5 in. (10–12.5 cm) flowers, produced mainly in spring and summer, although more can appear throughout the year if the plant is growing well. They vary in color, but are usually mid- to deep red with a long prominent central column.

Caring for plants
Keep the soil mix moist during spring to autumn. In winter, apply only sufficient water to prevent the soil mix from drying out. Fertilize with a high-potash liquid fertilizer, such as tomato fertilizer, every 2 weeks from spring to summer and once a month in autumn. If the plant begins to outgrow its position, it can be pruned hard in early spring.

Making new plants
Take 4-in. (10-cm)-long tip or heel cuttings in spring, and root in a sterile medium.

Hibiscus rosa-sinensis

Hippeastrum
Amaryllis, Knight's star lily

| 18 in. (47 cm) high | Normal room temperature | Direct sunlight |

*H*ippeastrum hybrids produce their 6 in. (15 cm) flowers in spring, in a wide range of colors from white through shades of pink, orange, and yellow to deep, velvety reds. Along with plain-colored petals, there are varieties with flecks, stripes, and different-colored edges. Up to 4 flowers are produced on the single stem, and a large bulb may produce 2 stems. The long, straplike leaves do not start to grow until the flower stalk is well advanced. Hippeastrum bulbs can be planted outside in the garden after flowering to be enjoyed for years to come. Once the flowers begin to fade, remove just the flowers and continue watering, leaving the stem and leaves to die down gradually. Before planting in the garden, work a long-lasting fertilizer into the soil around the bulbs to nourish them as they begin to grow. Unlike most other bulbs, they can also be brought indoors again in subsequent years.

Caring for plants
Keep the soil mix moist and fertilize with high-potash fertilizer every 2 weeks from after the flowers begin to fade until midsummer when the leaves die down.

Making new plants
Remove offsets in autumn. Sow seed at 60–65°F (16–18°C) once ripe.

Hippeastrum

Howea forsteriana
Kentia palm

| 8 ft. (2.4 m) high | Normal room temperature. Winter minimum 55°F (12°C) | Any, except deep shade |

This is a tolerant palm that seems to thrive in a range of indoor conditions. It makes a lovely specimen plant, particularly as it grows taller, but it needs plenty of room to grow well. The graceful, dark green foliage is almost flat in appearance, borne on tall, straight leaf stalks, with the many long leaflets drooping only slightly on each side of the raised midrib.

Caring for plants

Keep the soil mix thoroughly moist from spring to autumn. In winter, apply only sufficient water to prevent the mix from drying out. Water with standard liquid fertilizer once a month from spring to autumn. Wipe the leaves periodically with tepid water to remove dust.

Making new plants

Sow fresh seed—which is rarely produced on indoor plants—at a temperature of 80°F (25°C).

Howea forsteriana

Hoya lanceolata ssp. *bella*
Miniature wax plant

Stems can reach 18 in. (47 cm) long

Normal room temperature

Indirect sunlight

A trailing plant with thick, fleshy leaves and fragrant flowers, this looks wonderful in a hanging basket where the scent and the detail of the flowers can be appreciated. The stems are initially upright, arching only as they grow longer, and the dull green leaves are borne in pairs. The flowers appear in clusters of up to 10, each being star-shaped, with waxy white outer "petals" and a purple-red center. The plant exudes a milky latex when the stem is cut, although loss should not be excessive.

Caring for plants
Keep the soil mix moist from spring to autumn. In winter, apply only sufficient water to prevent the mix from drying out. Fertilize with high-potash fertilizer, such as tomato fertilizer, every 2 weeks during spring to autumn. Do not repot until absolutely necessary or disturb the plant once the flower buds begin to swell. After flowering, do not remove the flower spur because this is where the next flowers will also arise. Allow the flowers to fall naturally.

Making new plant
Take tip cuttings 3 in. (7.5 cm) long in spring or summer, and group them together, 3–5 to a pot.

Hoya lanceolata ssp. *bella*

Hyacinthus spp.
Hyacinth

8–12 in.
(20–30 cm)
high

Cool,
65°F
(18°C)

Indirect
sunlight

Hyacinths, forced to bloom for the indoors, can produce their brightly colored, highly scented flowers at any time from mid-December to March, according to when they are planted. Bulbs planted before September 15 will flower from mid-December onward. In order to get the best results, the bulbs used should be those marked on the packaging as "prepared." The most commonly available form is the traditional, single flower-stemmed *Hyacinthus orientalis*. Each flower stem carries up to 40 waxy flowers in colors ranging from pure white through cream, yellow, and orange to pink, red, violet, and blue over a period of 2–3 weeks. *H.* 'Multiflora White' has multiple stems and white flowers; *H.* 'Jan Bos' has red flowers. It is traditional to grow bulbs in open bowls of fibrous material, but many, particularly hyacinths, will also grow happily in a clear- or colored-glass container in both water and water-retaining gels.

Caring for plants
Keep the soil mix moist. Fertilizing is not necessary. The bulbs can be planted outside in the garden after flowering to be enjoyed for years to come. Once the flowers begin to fade, remove just the flower and continue watering, leaving the stem and leaves to die down gradually. Before planting in the garden, work a long-lasting fertilizer into the soil around the bulbs to nourish them as they begin to grow.

Making new plants
Remove offsets in summer while the bulb is dormant.

Hyacinthus orientalis

Hydrangea macrophylla
Hydrangea

24 in.
(60 cm)
high

Cool,
preferably
below 60°F
(15°C)

Indirect
sunlight

Mop-headed hydrangeas are grown indoors because they will tolerate being under cover. However, to grow well, they need cool, light, and airy conditions. They are well suited to growing in a cool greenhouse and form short, woody shrubs bearing large, oval leaves. The flowers are green in bud and open in a rounded cluster of blue, red, purple, pink, or white.

Caring for plants
Keep the soil mix thoroughly moist during spring to autumn. Water with standard liquid fertilizer every 2 weeks. The blue-flowered forms will need to be kept in an acid soil mix, or they will change color to pink or red. After flowering, discard the hydrangea or plant it in the garden because it is unlikely to bloom successfully indoors a second time.

Making new plants
This is only viable on a plant for outdoors. Take 4-in. (10-cm)-long tip cuttings in spring to summer and root in a sterile medium.

Hydrangea macrophylla

Hypoestes phyllostachya
Polka-dot plant

Limit to 12 in. (30 cm) high by pinching to keep the plant bushy

Normal room temperature

Indirect sunlight

Grown for their unusual foliage, these are small, shrublike plants that are usually grown for a year and then discarded when they grow too tall and woody. When they are young, the foliage is bushy, and the leaves are dark or olive green, conspicuously spotted with pink. Small lilac-colored flowers may be produced in spring, which will take energy from the leaves, so they may be pinched out.

Caring for plants
Keep the soil moist from spring to autumn. In winter, apply only sufficient water to prevent the mix from drying out. Water with standard liquid fertilizer every 2 weeks during spring to autumn. Keep in a well-lit area because too little light will cause the pink markings to become green.

Making new plants
Sow seed in spring or take 4-in. (10-cm)-long tip cuttings in spring to summer. Root in a sterile medium, and keep damp but not wet.

Hypoestes phyllostachya

Impatiens 'Exotic Fusion'
Impatiens

| 18 in. (47 cm) high | 24 in. (60 cm) spread | Normal room temperature | Direct sunlight (shade from midday summer sun) |

An unusual genetic mix of 2 interspecific hybrids gives these plants a completely different twist on the traditional impatiens. Their flower shape is similar to the standard form, but longer and with more pointed petals. Colors range from yellow through shades of orange to rose pink, all with a colored eye. They are reliable at producing clouds of pretty blooms and are easy to maintain, even flowering in deep shade. The plants form neat mounds, so they are ideal for containers, and flowering will continue throughout the year.

Caring for plants
Keep the potting soil thoroughly moist at all times. Water with standard liquid fertilizer at half strength once a week. Remove old flowers as they fade to maintain continuity of flowering and prevent disease.

Making new plants
Take softwood cuttings in spring, and root in a sterile medium.

Impatiens 'Exotic Fusion'

Impatiens 'Fiesta'
Impatiens

18 in.
(47 cm)
high

24 in.
(60 cm)
spread

Normal room
temperature

Direct sunlight
(shade from midday
summer sun)

Impatiens 'Fiesta' is an amazing collection of updated impatiens that grows quickly to form compact dome-shaped mounds of color. They are tolerant of most conditions, apart from drought, and naturally self-branch, so there is no need to pinch the tips. The small, multipetaled flowers are roselike in appearance and come in a range of bright colors, including shades of red, pink, lilac, and purple. Some, such as *Impatiens* 'Appleblossom' are multitonal and others, like *Impatiens* 'Ole Peppermint' also have variegated leaves. They are reliable and easy-to-maintain plants that will give color throughout much of the year in the home, porch, or greenhouse.

Caring for plants
Keep the soil mix thoroughly moist at all times. Water with standard liquid fertilizer at half strength once a week. Remove old flowers as they fade to maintain continuity of flowering and prevent disease.

Making new plants
Take softwood cuttings in spring, and root in a sterile medium.

Other varieties
Impatiens auricoma 'Jungle Gold' is a highly distinctive new impatiens with unusual orchidlike flowers carried in clusters above the glossy, dark green foliage. Each bloom is tubular-shaped and bright golden yellow with red markings in the throat.

Top: *Impatiens* 'Fiesta'; Bottom: *Impatiens auricoma* 'Jungle Gold'

Impatiens New Guinea hybrids
Impatiens

Up to
14 in.
(35 cm) high

Normal room
temperature

Indirect
sunlight

Larger than the traditional impatiens and almost shrubby in habit, the dramatic New Guinea hybrids bear the same characteristics: constant flowering from a young age, brittle, succulent-looking stems, and lush, fleshy foliage. They are more bold and colorful, with leaves that may be bright green, green splashed with yellow, or a bronze-red color. The flowers are larger, with a prominent spur, generally single, and come in many shades of red, pink, mauve, and white.

Caring for plants
Keep the soil mix moist from spring to autumn. In winter, apply only sufficient water to prevent the mix from drying out. Water with a standard liquid fertilizer every 2 weeks during spring to autumn. Too warm a location will cause rapid wilting, so stand pots on a tray of moist pebbles to increase humidity.

Making new plants
Take 4-in. (10-cm)-long tip cuttings in spring or summer and root in water or potting soil.

Impatiens New Guinea hybrids

Jasminum polyanthum
Jasmine

10 ft. (3 m) high or more if left unpruned

Cool room temperature. Stand outdoors in summer

Indirect sunlight

*J*asmine polyanthum is a graceful but vigorous climber that branches profusely as it is ages and it is easily trained. It will thrive in a pot, where it can be grown around a hoop or over a small trellis or in a greenhouse border, where it can be trained to cover a wall, larger trellis, or arch. The heavily scented clusters of tubular flowers are produced in winter and spring and are pink on the outside and white within. The glossy green leaves have 5–7 small leaflets.

Caring for plants

Keep the soil mix moist at all times. Water with standard liquid fertilizer once a month during summer to autumn. Keep jasmine under control by regular pruning and pinching out growing tips to encourage a bushy plant. It can be pruned hard after flowering, if necessary.

Making new plants

Take 4-in. (10-cm)-long tip or heel cuttings in summer, and root in a sterile medium.

Jasminum polyanthum

Justicia brandegeana (was *Beloperone guttata*)
Shrimp plant

10 ft. (3 m) high or more if left unpruned

Cool room temperature. Stand outdoors in summer

Indirect sunlight

The common name for this shrubby plant comes from the arching, 4-in. (10-cm)-long, shrimplike flowers, which are produced almost all year round. They are composed of many overlapping bracts in shades of yellow to brown, brick-red, or rose, surrounding a red- or purple-tipped white inner corolla. The stems are upright and woody, and the oval leaves are slightly downy. *Justica brandegeana* 'Yellow Queen' has bright yellow bracts.

Caring for plants
Keep the soil mix barely moist all year round. Water with standard liquid fertilizer once a month from spring to summer. Pinch out growing shoots regularly to encourage bushy growth, and cut the whole plant back by half its growth in spring to prevent it from becoming straggly.

Making new plants
Take 2–3-in. (5–7.5-cm)-long tip cuttings in spring or summer, and root in a sterile medium.

Justicia brandegeana (was Beloperone guttata)

Kalanchoe blossfeldiana
Flaming Katy

15 in.
(40 cm) high

Normal room
temperature

Direct
sunlight

This attractive, compact little plant normally flowers in the late winter and early spring for a period of about 3 months, but new hybrids and careful control of day length by the growers means that they can be brought into flower almost all year round. They are perennial plants, although they are frequently discarded after the flowers have faded. The small, tubular flowers are carried in crowded bunches in shades of red, orange, pink, or yellow, surrounded by rounded, glossy green leaves with slightly toothed edges.

Caring for plants

Keep the soil mix barely moist. Water with standard liquid fertilizer every 2 weeks while in flower. To keep the plant after flowering, allow it to rest for 6 weeks, give it minimal water and no fertilizer, and then resume. The subsequent flowering will be erratic, but the foliage is still attractive.

Making new plants

This is not generally attempted at home, since plants can be difficult to bring into flower and they are so readily available to buy.

Other varieties

Kalanchoe 'Tessa' has a pendant habit, making it ideal for use in a hanging basket or raised container. In late winter and early spring, bunches of tubular, orange-red flowers hang from the stems. Unlike *K. blossfeldiana*, *K.* 'Tessa' prefers indirect sunlight.

Kalanchoe blossfeldiana

Lagerstroemia indica
Crepe myrtle

| 9 ft. (2.7 m) high | 8 ft. (2.4 m) spread | Cool room temperature | Direct sunlight |

This is a spectacular upright, deciduous plant from central to eastern Asia, with peeling, gray-and-brown bark. The leaves are up to 3 in. (7.5 cm) long and are bronze as they first emerge, becoming dark green. During summer and autumn, tall panicles of flowers are produced on the shoot tips in white or shades of pink, red, or purple. Each flower is ¾–1 in. (2–2.5 cm) across and the panicle measures around 8 in. (20 cm) tall.

Caring for plants
Water freely during the growing season; then apply only enough water to prevent the soil mix from drying out. Feed with balanced liquid fertilizer every 8 weeks in spring and summer. Use a loam-based soil mix for best results.

Making new plants
Take semiripe cuttings in summer and plant in a loam-based fine soil mix.

Top and Bottom: *Lagerstroemia indica*

Lantana camara
Shrubby verbena, Yellow sage

18–24 in.
(47–60 cm)
high

Normal room
temperature.
Winter minimum
55°F (12°C)

Some direct sunlight
daily is essential
throughout year, or
plant will not flower.

This small shrubby plant has coarsely textured, dull, medium green leaves and bristly stems, but it erupts into color when it flowers throughout spring and summer. The numerous tubular flowers are produced in clusters on short stalks, opening progressively from the outside of the circle to the middle. An individual flower may be white, yellow, orange, pink, or red, usually with a brighter-colored eye, but the color changes and darkens as the flower ages, so that each cluster contains flowers of several different shades at once. *Lantana camara* 'Brasier' has bright red flowers, while *L. camara* 'Hybrida' is low-growing and has orange flowers.

Caring for plants
Keep thoroughly moist from spring to autumn. In winter, apply only sufficient water to prevent the soil mix from drying out. Water with standard liquid fertilizer every 2 weeks during spring to summer. Cut back after flowering. Young plants produce more flowers, so it is worth replacing the plant with cuttings every 2–3 years.

Making new plants
Sow seed in spring, or take 4-in. (10-cm)-long tip cuttings in spring or summer and root in a sterile medium.

Lantana camara

Lapageria rosea

Lapageria rosea
Chilean bell flower

| 10 ft. (3 m) high | Up to 10 ft. (3 m) spread | Cool room temperature | Indirect sunlight |

This acid-loving suckering climber has twining stems that produce oval-shaped, dark green leaves up to 5 in. (12.5 cm) in length. From summer through to late autumn, elongated, bell-shaped flowers are produced in clusters of up to 3 in the leaf axils. They are pink or red in color, with a fleshy texture. *Lapageria rosea* var. *albiflora* has pure white flowers and *L. rosea* 'Nash Court' has flowers of pink with a cerise mottling. This plant is ideal when grown on a frame or trellis in a garden room, cool greenhouse, or well-lit porch.

Caring for plants
Water moderately and allow the soil mix to dry slightly between waterings. Water with standard liquid tomato fertilizer at half strength every 2 weeks from spring to late summer. This plant needs to be grown in an ericaceous soil mix.

Making new plants
Take semiripe cuttings in late summer or remove suckers in spring as they emerge, and plant in an ericaceous soil mix.

Laurus nobilis
Bay

Up to
10 ft. (3 m)
high

Normal room
temperature

Sunlight

Ultimately a large evergreen shrub or small tree, this woody plant originates in the Mediterranean area. It has aromatic, oval-shaped, glossy mid-green leaves and clusters of small yellow flowers that appear in spring. It can be clipped into a variety of ornamental shapes, and the dried leaves are commonly used in cooking. Although it is often grown in the garden, it also makes a good plant for a porch or greenhouse, especially when it is clipped into a formal shape.

Caring for plants
Keep moist in spring and summer, and spray the leaves with water occasionally to keep them clean and shining. Keep the plant out of drafts.

Making new plants
Take a cutting with a heel around 5 in. (12.5 cm) long in early summer. Alternatively, layer established plants in summer. Insert several cuttings in a sterile medium in pans, but transplant individually when the roots are established.

Laurus nobilis

Leptospermum scoparium
Manuka, Tea tree

Up to
10 ft. (3 m)
high

Tolerant of a
range of
temperature.
Winter min.
40°F (4°C)

Direct sunlight,
except midday
in summer.
Cool light.

Tea tree is a pretty flowering and woody evergreen shrub with glossy, aromatic leaves that are covered with a sheen of fine, silky hairs as they emerge. The 5-petaled flowers are usually white, although there are cultivars available in shades of pink and red. It is almost hardy outdoors in milder areas, but will thrive in a cool greenhouse. *Leptospermum scoparium* 'Burgundy Queen' is a form with deep red flowers, *L. scoparium* 'Cherry Brandy' has deep red-bronze leaves and cerise flowers. *L. scoparium* 'Keatleyi' has large pink flowers, and the new shoots are red and silky.

Caring for plants
Keep the soil mix moist in spring to autumn but drier in winter. Water with standard liquid fertilizer once a month during spring to summer. Keep the plant bushy by pinching the tips of the shoots after flowering.

Making new plants
Take 4-in. (10-cm)-long tip or heel cuttings in spring or summer, and root in a sterile medium.

Top and Bottom: *Leptospermum scoparium*

Leucospermum cordifolium
Pincushion

36 in.
(90 cm)
high

36 in.
(90 cm)
spread

Cool room
temperature

Direct
sunlight

This is a spreading shrub with a dome-shaped habit, originally from South Africa. The leaves are mid-green and oblong in shape, up to 3 in. (7.5 cm) in length, covered with down when they are young but becoming smooth with age. From early spring to midsummer, solitary orange, crimson, or yellow flower heads up to 5 in. (12 cm) wide are produced on the tips of the stems. They are spherical in shape, composed of many inward-arching spikes—actually styles—hence, the common name of pincushion.

Caring for plants
Keep the soil mix moist, but allow to dry slightly between waterings. Water with standard liquid fertilizer once a month during spring and early summer. Needs to be grown in an ericaceous soil mix.

Making new plants
Take semiripe cuttings in summer, and plant in ericaceous potting soil.

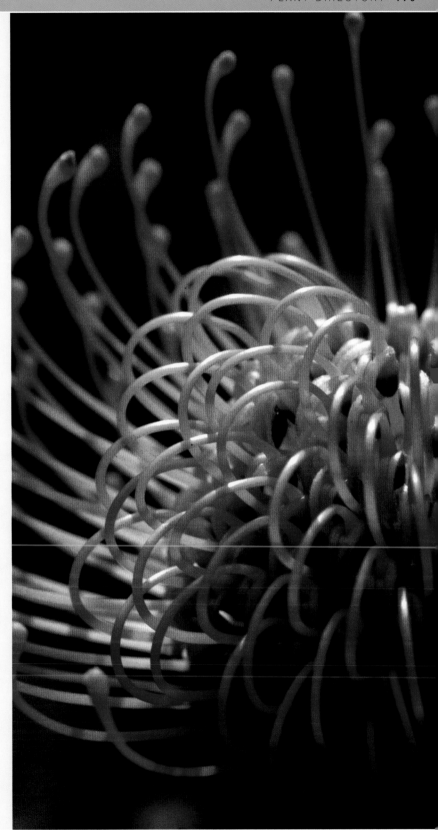

Leucospermum cordifolium

Licuala grandis
Licuala

10 ft.
(3 m) high

Minimum
60°F (15°C)

Indirect sunlight
or partial shade

This is a small palm with an upright trunk of up to 10 ft. (3 m) in height, covered in fibrous leaf bases. The long-stalked leaf blades are arranged spirally around the upper part of the stem, and each blade is rounded and glossy, reaching up to 36 in. (90 cm) across on a mature plant. They are pale to mid-green in color, with wavy edges, and divided into 3 wedge-shaped segments. The green-white flowers are produced on long, drooping spikes in summer. This is a good plant for a warm greenhouse where it can be grown in a border.

Caring for plants
Keep the soil mix thoroughly moist from spring to autumn and drier in winter. Mist regularly in summer, especially if the temperature is high. Water with standard liquid fertilizer once a month during spring to autumn.

Making new plants
Sow seed in spring at 75°F (25°C), or take suckers from an established plant and plant in a fast-draining potting soil.

Licuala grandis

Lilium regale
Regal lily

48 in.
(120 cm)
high

Cool room
temperature (but
above freezing at
night in spring)

Indirect
sunlight

The Lily family is a large one, comprising around 100 bulbous perennial plants. These vary considerably in height, flower size, shape, and color, but they share certain characteristics. The bulb is always made up of fleshy white or yellow scales, although these may turn purple when exposed to light. *L. regale* is a fairly tall plant for indoors, and like other members of the Lily family, it grows best in a cool spot, perhaps a porch or shady greenhouse. The trumpet-shaped flowers are produced in summer and are white with a yellow throat, heavily scented, and up to 6 in. (15 cm) across. Lily pollen can mark polished surfaces when it falls.

Caring for plants

Keep the soil mix thoroughly moist at all times as the plant grows and flowers. After flowering, reduce watering to keep the mix just moist as the plant dies down. Fertilize with a high-potash fertilizer, such as tomato fertilizer, every 2 weeks from when the flower begins to fade until the leaves die down, especially if the bulb is to be grown indoors again the following season. Bring lilies into flower the next season by repotting in autumn after the foliage has died down.

Making new plants

Take healthy scales from the bulb before planting. Remove them cleanly by breaking them from the bulb. Place them in a plastic bag of moist peat moss and put in a warm, dark place. Within 6–8 weeks, tiny new bulbils will begin to form on the lower edges of the scales. These can be potted and grown in their own right.

Lilium regale

Lilium speciosum
Japanese lily

| 36–48 in. (90–120 cm) high | Cool (but above freezing at night in spring) | Indirect sunlight |

The bowl-shaped flowers of *Lilium speciosum* are produced in summer and are white with red markings. They are 3–5 in. (7.5–12.5 cm) across and highly scented. Lily bulbs can be bought throughout the winter and spring, but make sure that they are plump and glossy, not shriveled or dry looking. Plant immediately, keeping the "nose" or tip of the bulb just under the surface of the compost.

Caring for plants

As the plant grows and flowers, keep the soil mix thoroughly moist at all times. After flowering, reduce watering to a minimum as the plant dies down. Fertilize with a high-potash fertilizer, such as tomato fertilizer, every 2 weeks from when the flower begins to fade until the leaves die down. This is particularly important if the bulb is to be grown indoors again the following season. Lilies can be brought into flower the next season by repotting in autumn after the foliage has died down.

Making new plants

Take healthy scales from the bulb before planting. Remove them cleanly by breaking them from the bulb. Place them in a plastic bag of moist peat moss and put in a warm, dark place. Within 6–8 weeks, tiny new bulbil will begin to form on the lower edges of the scales. These can be repotted and grown in their own right.

Top and Bottom: *Lilium speciosum*

Lithops marmorata
Living stones

1¼ in.
(3 cm)
high

2 in.
(5 cm)
spread

Normal
room
temperature

Direct sunlight
(shade from
midday
summer sun)

This is a peculiar little succulent perennial that originates from South Africa. It has a thick, soft rootstock and inverse cone-shaped upper parts, each composed of a pair of very fleshy gray-green or beige "leaves" ¾–1¼ in. (2–3 cm) across, with a fissure running across the middle. The upper surface is almost translucent with a panel of spots or patches. Scented white daisylike flowers are produced from the fissure during late summer and autumn, sometimes followed by small fleshy capsules containing seeds. Grow in a wide container to create a conversation piece when the plants flower.

Caring for plants
Water freely from spring until autumn; then apply only enough water to prevent the soil mix from drying out. Water with standard liquid tomato fertilizer at half strength monthly from spring to late summer.

Making new plants
Remove offsets in early summer or sow seed at 66–75°F (19–24°C).

Lithops marmorata

Lotus berthelotii
Coral gem, Parrot's beak, Pelican's beak

Stems to 24 in. (60 cm)

Winter minimum 50°F (10°C)

Some direct sunlight

This is a perennial subshrub with trailing gray stems covered with deeply divided silvery gray leaves. The 1½-in. (4-cm)-long flowers are produced in spring and summer, either singly or in pairs, and are orange-red to scarlet or purple and shaped like a claw or beak, which gives rise to the various common names. Although hardy outdoors in some milder areas, Lotus may still need winter protection, and it will grow well in a sunroom or greenhouse, where the beautiful flowers can be fully appreciated.

Caring for plants
Keep the potting soil moist from spring to autumn and drier in winter. Water with standard liquid fertilizer once a month in spring to autumn. Cut back, if necessary, immediately after flowering. Some direct sunlight is essential to ripen the shoots ready for flowering.

Making new plants
Sow seed in spring at 65–75°F (18–24°C), or take 4-in. (10-cm)-long tip or heel cuttings in late spring or summer.

Lotus berthelotii

Mammillaria zeilmanniana
Rose pincushion

4 in.
(10 cm)
across in
4 years

Normal warm
room
temperature
spring-
autumn.

Direct
sunlight

Mammillaria is the largest genus of the Cactus family, comprised of more than 300 species. They are different from other cacti in that they do not have ribs; they have spirally arranged swellings, tubercles, each with an areole at the tip bearing—in this case—clusters of 4 main red-brown spines surrounded by 15–18 bristly white radial spines. Initially a solitary plant, it grows to form a cluster of glossy green, globe-shaped stems. The violet-pink or purple flowers are produced in spring in a ring around the top of the plant. Because the flowers are produced from part of the stem that grew the previous year, a poor growth season means less likelihood of a good display of flowers the following spring.

Caring for plants
Keep the soil mix moist from spring to autumn, but during winter, apply only sufficient water to prevent the mix from drying out. During the winter rest period, try to keep the temperature at 50ºF (10ºC) and no lower than 40ºF (5ºC). Fertilize with standard liquid tomato fertilizer once a month during spring and summer.

Making new plants
Allow the pulp from the berries to dry; then pick out the seeds. Sow seed or detach offsets by cutting or pulling away from the parent plant, drying for 24 hours, then planting.

Mammillaria zeilmanniana

Mandevilla sanderi (was *Dipladenia sanderi*)
Brazilian jasmine

| Up to 10 ft. (3 m) high if left unpruned | Normal room temperature | Indirect sunlight |

A woody climber this plant supports itself by winding its stems around a support. The leathery leaves are a glossy mid-green, borne in pairs, and up to 2 in. (5 cm) long. Throughout the late spring, summer, and early autumn, the flowers appear on the new growth in clusters of 3–5. They are large and showy, trumpet-shaped, up to 3 in. (7.5 cm) across, and a glorious rose-pink with a yellow throat. The flowers are produced when the plant is still young, and regular pinching can be used to encourage a bushy plant rather than a tall one. *Mandevilla sanderi* 'Rosea' has larger leaves, with bronze beneath, and flowers to 3½ in. (8 cm) across, which are salmon pink with a yellow throat.

Caring for plants
Keep moist during spring to autumn, but in winter, apply only sufficient water to prevent the soil mix drying out. Water with standard liquid fertilizer every 2 weeks from spring to summer. Flowers are produced only on the current year's growth, so do not prune until autumn; then cut back most of the newest shoots to encourage the production of more for the following spring.

Making more plants
Take 4-in. (10-cm)-long tip cuttings from new growth in spring, root in a sterile medium, and keep in a temperature of 75–78°F (24–25°C).

Other varieties
Mandevilla x *amabilis* 'Alice du Pont' produces large clusters of up to 20 funnel-shaped, bright rose-pink flowers throughout the summer.

Mandevilla sanderi

Maranta leuconeura
Prayer plant

12 in.
(30 cm)
high

Normal
room
temperature

Partial
shade

The common name of this plant is derived
from its habit of folding its leaves together
at night. It is grown primarily for its striking
foliage. The leaves are oval shaped up to 5 in.
(12.5 cm) long, and a lustrous dark green,
marked with gray or maroon, and veined silver,
red, or purple above and gray-green or maroon
below. The white or violet flowers are small and
insignificant. *Maranta leuconeura*
Erythroneura—known as the Herringbone
plant—has green-black leaves with scarlet veins
and a lime-green zone along the midrib. *M.
leuconeura* Kerchoveana—Rabbit's foot—has
gray-green leaves with a row of purple-brown-to-
olive blotches along each side of the midrib.

Caring for plants
Keep the soil mix thoroughly moist in spring to
autumn and drier in winter. Water with
standard liquid fertilizer once a month during
spring to summer. Do not allow water to splash
onto the leaves or it will cause discoloration.

Making more plants
Divide large clumps in spring, or take 4-in.
(10-cm)-long cuttings with 3–4 leaves in spring
or summer. Root in a sterile medium.

Maranta leuconeura

Mentha spicata
Mint

24–36 in.
(60–90 cm)
high

Normal
room
temperature

Sunlight or
partial
shade

There are numerous mint species, but *Mentha spicata* is perhaps the most common. It is an invasive hardy perennial plant with narrow, pointed leaves. If left to flower, it grows purple spikes held well above the leaves. The leaves are used in mint sauce, salads, and drinks. Pick them before flowering, and use them fresh, dried, frozen, or chopped finely and infused in vinegar.

Caring for plants
Grow in pots on a sunny windowsill and water regularly. Pinch out the growing shoots to use in cooking and to keep the plant bushy.

Making more plants
Like other species of mint, this one is self-propagating, spreading all over the place if not kept in check.

Mentha spicata

Microlepia strigosa
Microlepia

36 in.
(90 cm)
high

Normal
room
temperature

Indirect
sunlight
or partial
shade

This is a fern in the traditional sense, with creeping rhizomes that send up graceful, deeply divided fronds as long as 30 x 12 in. (75 x 30 cm). Each is divided into 2–3 pinnae that are oval- to lance-shaped, with short, coarse hairs on the veins. The pinnae are further divided into 20 x 1½ in. (4 cm) pinnules, which are oblong in shape with a notch at the tip and toothed or lobed along the edges. The leafstalks are up to 14 in. (35 cm) long and covered with coarse hairs.

Caring for plants
Keep the soil mix thoroughly moist in spring to autumn and drier in winter. Maintain high humidity by misting regularly or standing the pot on a tray of moist pebbles. Water with standard liquid fertilizer once a month during spring to autumn.

Making new plants
Divide rhizomes in spring or sow spores at 70°F (20°C).

Microlepia strigosa

Miltoniopsis hybrid

Miltoniopsis hybrids
Pansy orchid

9 in. (23 cm) high	9 in. (23 cm) spread	Normal room temperature	Indirect sunlight

These stunning orchids are epiphytic, with ovoid pseudobulbs and narrow, straplike leaves up to 8 in. (20 cm) long. They produce fragrant, long-lasting flowers from late winter to early summer that closely resemble the garden pansy in both shape and markings. Each is around 3 in. (7.5 cm) across, and there may be up to 6 flowers in each raceme. They are colored white or shades of red from almost brown to quite vivid, and most have markings in white, orange, or yellow.

Caring for plants
Water freely from spring until autumn; then apply only enough water to prevent the soil mix from drying out. Needs high humidity, but do not mist onto the foliage, because it quickly becomes spotted. Stand the container on a saucer of damp pebbles. Fertilize with standard liquid fertilizer once a month during spring and early summer.

Making new plants
Divide when the plant outgrows its pot, potting the pseudobulbs separately.

Monstera deliciosa
Swiss cheese plant

10 ft. (3 m) or more high

Normal room temperature

Indirect sunlight

In its native habitat, the monstera will scramble up the trunks and along the branches of large trees, anchoring itself into place by means of strong aerial roots, which also serve to take in moisture and nutrients. It matures into a large plant, with heart-shaped leaves up to 18 in. (47 cm) across on 12 in. (30 cm) stalks. The common name arises from the leaves, which are undivided on a young plant but which gradually become deeply incised between the veins, with holes in the remaining sections.

Caring for plants
Keep barely moist all year round. Train the stem against a moss pole to allow the aerial roots to anchor and take in moisture as they would in the wild. Water with standard liquid fertilizer once a month from spring to autumn.

Making new plants
Take tip cuttings of 2 leaves in spring, stem cuttings of a single node with a short length of stem, layer or air layer.

Monstera deliciosa

Murraya paniculata
Orange jasmine, Satinwood, Chinese box

10–12 ft.
(3-3.5 m)
high

Minimum
55–60°F
(12–15°C)

Partial shade,
but with some
direct sunlight

Ultimately, murraya will form a large, strongly aromatic evergreen tree or shrub ideal for a greenhouse. It is grown for its appearance and for flavoring curries. The dark green leaves are glossy and smooth, divided into 3 or more pinnae, and each rectangular leaflet is up to 2 in. (5 cm) long. The small, fragrant white flowers are produced in densely packed terminal clusters throughout the year and are followed by oval orange-red fruit.

Caring for plants
Keep the soil mix thoroughly moist in spring to autumn and drier in winter. Water with standard liquid fertilizer once a month during spring to summer. Prune in late winter, if necessary.

Making new plants
Sow seed in spring, or take semiripe tip cuttings in summer.

Murraya paniculata

Musa acuminata
Banana

84 in.
(210 cm)

Tolerant of a
range of
temperatures.
Winter
minimum
55°F (12°C)

Direct sunlight,
indirect sunlight,
or partial shade,
depending on
variety.

Many varieties of the banana grow much too big for even a large greenhouse, but *Musa acuminata* 'Dwarf Cavendish' is a more compact form and will often produce small edible fruits. Each green-brown, suckering pseudostem is formed from overlapping leaf sheaths and the palmlike leaves grow to 36 in. (90 cm) or more in length. The tubular, pendulous flowers have pointed red-purple bracts on a brown-haired central peduncle from which the young fruit curve upward. The banana will grow in a greenhouse border or in a large container.

Caring for plants
Keep the soil mix thoroughly moist in spring to autumn and moist in winter. Water with standard liquid fertilizer once a month during spring to summer. For the production of fruit, keep the temperature above 65°F (18°C), even at night.

Making new plants
Detach rooted suckers from the mature plant in summer.

Musa acuminata

Muscari azureum
Grape hyacinth

| 4 in. (10 cm) high | 2 in. (5 cm) spread | Cool room temperature | Bright indirect light |

These small perennial plants originate from Turkey. They grow from bulbs, producing clusters of fleshy, upright, narrow, gray-green leaves up to 8 in. (20 cm) long. In spring, they produce bell-shaped, vivid sky blue flowers with a darker stripe in clusters up to 1¼ in. (3 cm) long on upright stems. The plants are hardy, but like many bulbs, they can be used indoors for display purposes. Muscari were very popular with the Victorians, who grew them in mossed pyramids or inverted cones as table centerpieces.

Caring for plants
Keep the soil mix thoroughly moist. Water with standard liquid tomato fertilizer at half strength once a week. Can be planted outdoors after flowering.

Making more plants
Sow seed in autumn, or divide clumps and remove offsets in summer.

Muscari azureum

Narcissus
Narcissus, Daffodil

Variable | Cool room temperature | Direct sunlight

The genus *Narcissus* is enormous and highly varied in both size and flower form, ranging from tiny 4 in. (10 cm) dwarf types to traditional, tall garden varieties of 24 in. (60 cm) high. Many can be brought into flower with great success indoors, especially in a porch or greenhouse where they can enjoy cool, well-lit conditions away from damaging frosts and high winds. The flowers come in shades of yellow, white, orange, cream, and, more recently, pink, and can be single or clustered, with single or double petals and varying lengths and shapes of trumpet. Recommended varieties as houseplants are *Narcissus* 'Tete-a-Tete', 6–12 in. (15–30 cm) high with yellow, multiheaded flowers; *N.* 'Sundial', 6–12 in. (15–30 cm) high with wide, yellow flowers; *N.* 'Paperwhite' which is 12–18 in. (30–47 cm) high and has white, highly scented flowers; and *N.* 'Bridal Crown', 12–18 in. (30–47 cm) high with cream double flowers.

Caring for plants
Keep the soil mix moist at all times. Apply standard liquid fertilizer at half strength once a week from flower opening until the leaves turn yellow.

Making more plants
Remove offsets as the leaves die down in late spring or in early autumn as you plant the bulbs.

Narcissus papyraceus

Neoregelia carolinae 'Tricolor'
Blushing bromeliad

| 8–12 in. (20–30 cm) high | 15–24 in. (40–60 cm) spread | Normal room temperature | Indirect sunlight |

This is an epiphytic bromeliad, originating from South America, with open rosettes of up to 20 strap-shaped leaves growing from a basal rosette. Each is striped green, white, and rosy pink and grows to 15–24 in. (40–60 cm) long. During the summer, long-lasting, tubular-shaped, violet-to-lavender flowers are produced from the center of the rosette, usually causing an increase in the color intensity of the leaves.

Caring for plants
Keep the soil mix thoroughly moist and keep the rosette cup filled with soft water from spring to autumn. Water sparingly in winter. Water with standard liquid fertilizer once a month during spring and summer. Cut flowered rosettes off at the base to encourage subsequent rosettes to flower. Grow in an epiphytic bromeliad medium.

Making new plants
Separate and pot offsets in spring or summer.

Neoregelia carolinae 'Tricolor'

Nephrolepis exaltata 'Bostoniensis' Boston fern

| 18 in. (45 cm) high | 36 in. (90 cm) wide at 5 years | Normal room temperature all year round | Indirect sunlight or warm partial shade (not deep shade) |

This is a lush, graceful fern, with long, arching fronds that makes a lovely specimen plant on a pedestal or in a hanging basket. In the right conditions, the fronds can reach 48-in. (120-cm) long, and are a rich mid-green, with numerous pinnae occurring alternately on each side of the midrib. As the plant matures, 2 rows of brown sporangia become apparent on the underside of each pinna, on either side of the central vein.

Caring for plants

Keep the soil mix thoroughly moist at all times. In higher temperatures, dry air will cause browning of the pinnae, so be sure to increase humidity by standing the pot on a tray of moist pebbles. Water with standard liquid fertilizer every 2 weeks from spring to autumn.

Making more plants

Furry runners grow from the rhizome, and plantlets develop at their tips. Remove the plantlet once it has rooted by severing the runner with a sharp knife. Spore propagation is not easy, because viability is variable.

Nephrolepis exaltata 'Bostoniensis'

Nerium oleander
Oleander

Up to
72 in.
(180 cm)
high

Normal room
temperature
spring–autumn

Direct
sunlight

A large evergreen shrub with leathery, dark green leaves, this is grown for its display of beautiful, often fragrant, funnel-shaped flowers. These are produced in terminal clusters and can be single, semidouble, or fully double, according to the variety, in shades of white, cream, yellow, apricot, salmon, copper, pink, red, carmine, and purple. Individual flowers can be up to 2 in. (5 cm) across, and they are borne in groups of 6–8. This is an ideal plant for a sunny windowsill while it is small and for a well-lit greenhouse as it grows. *The whole plant is poisonous (sap, flowers, and seeds), so handle with extreme caution and wash your hands thoroughly after contact.*

Caring for plants
Keep the soil mix thoroughly moist from spring to autumn, but barely moist in winter. Allowing the plant to dry out as the flowers form will result in the buds being shed. Water with standard liquid fertilizer every 2 weeks during spring to summer. Keep at normal room temperature from spring to autumn but below 60°F (15°C) and above 45°F (7°C) in winter for the rest period.

Making more plants
Take tip cuttings up to 6 in. (15 cm) long in summer, and root them in water or potting soil.

Nerium oleander

Nertera granadensis
Bead plant

¾ in.
(2 cm)
high

8 in.
(20 cm)
spread

Normal
room
temperature

Indirect
sunlight

T his is a mat-forming, mosslike perennial, with oval-shaped, bright green leaves, that originates from Mexico. In summer, it produces small, stemless, bell-shaped yellowish green flowers ⅛ in. (3 mm) across, followed by copious tiny spherical berries that are glossy orange or red. This is a good plant for a wide container on a low table where space is limited because the bright, shiny berries are immediately attractive.

Caring for plants
Water freely from spring until autumn; then apply only enough water to prevent the soil mix from drying out. Water with standard liquid fertilizer once a month during spring and summer. This plant prefers to grow in loamless soil mix.

Making more plants
Divide mature plants or sow seed at 55–61°F (13–16°C) in spring.

Top and Bottom: *Nertera granadensis*

Nidularium fulgens
Bird's nest bromeliad

| 15 in. (40 cm) high | Up to 24 in. (60 cm) spread | Normal room temperature | Indirect sunlight |

This is a spreading, rhizomatous, and epiphytic bromeliad with rosettes of up to 20 leaves. These are strap-shaped, sharply toothed, and bright pale green, up to 15 in. (40 cm) long and slightly scaly underneath. Clusters of 2-in. (5-cm)-long, tubular white flowers with purplish tips are produced in a mass—or bird's nest—of bright red bracts in the center of the rosette in summer.

Caring for plants
Keep the rosette cup filled with soft water from spring until autumn. Water freely with soft water from spring until autumn; then apply only enough water to prevent the soil mix from drying out. Grow in an epiphytic bromeliad soil mix and water with standard liquid fertilizer once a month during spring and summer.

Making more plants
Separate and pot offsets in spring or summer, and grow in an epiphytic bromeliad potting soil.

Top and Bottom: *Nidularium fulgens*

Nolina recurvata (syn. *Beaucarnea recurvata*)
Pony tail, Elephant foot tree, Bottle palm

Up to 6–7 ft. (2 m) high | Direct sunlight | Normal room temperature, winter minimum 50°F (10°C)

An unusual plant, this eventually becomes a large tree in the wild, with a flask-shaped trunk, swollen at the base, giving rise to two of its common names. It branches rarely as it ages and has clusters of long, dark green leaves in terminal rosettes. Each leaf curves downward, with a pronounced channel and slightly toothed edges. It is this plume of foliage that gives the plant its common name of "Pony tail."

Caring for plants
Keep the soil mix moist in spring to autumn. In winter, apply only sufficient water to prevent the mix from drying out. The swollen base is used for storing water, so this is a plant that that can cope with occasional neglect. Water with standard liquid fertilizer once a month during spring to summer.

Making more plants
Detach offsets in spring, and repot individually.

Nolina recurvata (syn. *Beaucarnea recurvata*)

Ocimum basilicum

Ocimum basilicum
Basil

20 in.
(50 cm)
high

Warm room
temperature

Direct
sunlight

This is a half-hardy annual herb with large, soft leaves that grows well on a sunny windowsill. Tiny, white, purple-tinged flowers are borne in midsummer. The leaves are used in tomato pasta dishes, salads, vinegars, and pesto. Young leaves can either be picked and used fresh, or frozen, dried, or bottled in oil for future use. Sweet basil can be grown outdoors, but keeping a pot on a sunny windowsill ensures a fresh supply of leaves for cooking. This is also a good patio or window box plant.

Caring for plants
Needs a minimum of 5 hours of sun a day. Water just enough to keep the soil mix moist. Pick leaves regularly to ensure a fresh supply.

Making more plants
Sow seed in a rich soil mix of seed and potting compost, and thin when the seedlings are a few inches high.

Odontoglossum spp.
Orchid

| 12–36 in. (30–90 cm) high | 10–12 in. (25–30 cm) spread | Normal room. During winter rest period, keep at about 60°F (15°C) | Indirect sunlight |

This beautiful, evergreen, open-flowered orchid is naturally epiphytic and grows on another plant to make use of moisture in the air. There are many hybrids, with flower colors including crisp whites and shades of yellow, green, red, and chestnut brown. Each flower has broad petals and distinctive central "lips" that may be spotted or splashed with a contrasting color. As many as 12 flowers may be produced on single upright or arching stems up to 30 in. (75 cm) long, and each individual bloom may be up to 3 in. (7.5 cm) across. The mid-green, straplike leaves are produced from a pseudobulb—it is actually a rhizome—at the base.

Caring for plants
This species of orchid needs high humidity, so water and mist daily. Water with standard liquid fertilizer once a week. Grow in fine-grade epiphytic orchid mix.

Making more plants
Divide when the plant fills the pot. Plant the sections in fine-grade epiphytic orchid mix.

Top and Bottom: *Odontoglossum*

Opuntia humifusa
(syn. *O. compressa*)
Prickly pear

| 8–12 in. (20–30 cm) high | Up to 36 in. (90 cm) spread | Normal room temperature | Direct sunlight |

This clump-forming perennial cactus is unusual in that, with a little winter protection, it is hardy outdoors in many areas. It also makes a dramatic indoor plant where space allows. Its large, oval pads spread out sideways, growing to fill a wide, shallow container. The plant's attractions are that it bears two spines than most cacti and it produces a profuse display of stunning funnel-shaped, bright yellow flowers of 1½–2½ in. (4–6 cm) across in late spring and early summer. These are sometimes followed by purple or red fruits. This is an ideal plant for a sunny spot or greenhouse. The fruits are edible, though not tasty.

Caring for plants
Water freely from spring until autumn; then apply only enough water to prevent the soil mix from drying out. Water with standard liquid fertilizer once a month from spring to autumn.

Making more plants
Sow presoaked seed in spring at 70°F (21°C), or carefully separate stem segments and root in a cactus medium.

Other varieties
Opuntia brasiliensis is a desert-type cactus from South America, which will ultimately become treelike in its natural habitat; but in a container, it remains much more compact.

Top: *Opuntia humifusa*; Bottom: *Opuntia brasiliensis*

Opuntia microdasys
Prickly pear

12 in.
(30 cm)

12 in.
(30 cm) in
10 years

Normal room
temperature,
with a winter
minimum of
50°F (10°C)

Direct
sunlight

This opuntia takes its common name from its spiny pear-shaped fruit and it naturally forms shrubby thickets 15–24 in. (40–60 cm) in height. Indoors, it tends to remain much more compact. This is one desert cactus that does not have ridges. Instead it has velvety-looking stem segments, reaching 2½–6 in. (6–15 cm) in length. These are flattened and oval in shape, and covered at regular intervals all over by areoles packed with tiny golden or white "glochids"—hooked bristles. This variety is grown for its shape and appearance rather than its yellow flowers, which do not always appear on indoor specimens. The glochids from this plant are easily detached by even the most gentle touch and quickly penetrate the skin. They are highly irritating and should be removed as quickly as possible with adhesive tape.

Caring for plants
Keep the soil mix moist but never wet, from spring to autumn. In winter, apply only enough water to prevent the mix from drying out. Water with liquid tomato fertilizer every 2 weeks during spring to summer.

Making more plants
Segments can be detached by cutting or pulling from the parent plant in spring or summer. Allow to dry for up to 3 days; then plant into small pots of cactus mix.

Opuntia microdasys

Origanum vulgare
Marjoram or Oregano

8 in. (20 cm) high

Normal room temperature

Direct sunlight

Marjoram and oregano are members of the same species of plants. Both are hardy herbaceous perennials, and both need warmth and bright light in order to grow well. *Origanum vulgare* is called wild majoram in America; it has red stems and spreads by tiny rhizomes. The pungent leaves can be used fresh, dried, or frozen, particularly in Italian, egg, and cheese dishes. Although normally a garden plant, it can be grown in a pot on a sunny windowsill or in a window box to provide fresh herbs for cooking throughout the year.

Caring for plants
Keep the soil mix moist throughout the year, but do not overwater. Water with a little half-strength fertilizer once a month.

Making more plants
Sow seed in spring in potting soil, take cuttings in summer, or divide the roots of mature plants in autumn.

Origanum vulgare

Pachycereus schottii
No common name

Up to 84 in.
(210 cm)
high

36 in.
(90 cm)
spread

Normal
room
temperature

Direct
sunlight

This is an upright, columnar cactus originating from Arizona and Mexico. It has dark green stems, each with up to 9 ribs. The woolly gray areoles produce sharp black spines that fade to gray in groups of 4–7 with one central spine. Once the plant has matured, it may produce flowers in summer from a hairy, woody growth on the stem. These are nocturnal and funnel-shaped, in red, pink, or white, with green outside, and may be followed by spherical fleshy fruits containing black seeds. This plant will give height to a collection of cacti in a desert-type display, but in the wild, it can grow taller than 84 in. (210 cm).

Caring for plants
Water moderately in spring to summer and allow to dry slightly between waterings. At all other times, water sparingly. Water with standard liquid fertilizer once a month during spring and early summer.

Making more plants
Take stem tip cuttings in summer, or sow seed at 66–75°F (19–24°C) in spring.

Pachycereus schottii

Paphiopedilum spp.
Slipper orchid

18 in.
(47 cm)
high

Normal
room
temperature

Indirect
sunlight

This is a stemless, terrestrial orchid, with thick, fleshy leaves arising from a short rhizome. The waxy flowers are borne, usually singly, at the top of a long, slender stalk in shades of green, pink, bronze, maroon and purple. They have a pouchlike lip that is shaped like the front of a slipper; hence, the common name. Each flower lasts between 8–12 weeks, and the flowering season is between autumn and spring.

Caring for plants

Keep moist throughout the year except for the 6-month period after flowering, when only sufficient water should be applied to prevent the mix from drying out. The roots will quickly rot if the plant is overwatered. Fertilize with a foliar spray once a month, except during the rest period after flowering. If the flower is tending to droop, tie it to a thin cane inserted into the pot close to the plant.

Making more plants

Divide mature plants at the end of the flowering season.

Paphiopedilum

Parodia chrysacanthion
No common name

5 in. (12.5 cm) high

4 in. (10 cm) spread after 10 years

Normal room temperature. Winter min. 10°C (50°F)

Direct sunlight

This is a globe-shaped desert cactus that grows slowly both indoors and in the wild. It is covered in spirally arranged tubercles, each topped with an areole bearing 30–40 straight pale yellow spines ½ in. (12 mm) long, and 3–5 golden-yellow spines of up to 1 in. (2.5 cm) in length. The very apex of the plant is woolly and tufted with erect spines. The yellow flowers appear in spring and are up to 1 in. (2.5 cm) across.

Caring for plants
Keep the soil mix moist, but never wet, during spring to autumn. In winter, apply only enough water to prevent the mix from drying out. Water with liquid tomato fertilizer once a month in spring to summer. If the roots show any sign of rotting when the plant is repotted, cut any damaged tissue back to healthy growth and repot.

Making more plants
Take offsets, if any are present during summer and allow them to dry for up to 3 days before potting into cactus mix. If no offsets form, raise them from seed.

Parodia chrysacanthion

Parodia concinna
(was *Notocactus apricus*)
No common name

1¼–1½ in.
(3–4 cm)
high

4 in.
(10 cm)
spread

Normal room
temperature.
Winter min.
50°F (10°C)

Direct
sunlight

This nonbranching, globe-shaped desert cactus is grown for both its attractive spines and its display of lemon yellow flowers in spring. It is ridged lengthwise with 15–32 low ribs, each having areoles set along it bearing twisted, hairlike spines in clusters of 9–25 shorter, pale yellow, radial spines and 4–6, or more, central red-brown spines. The apex of the plant is depressed inward, and the funnel-shaped flowers appear around this indentation. They are 2–3 in. (5–7.5 cm) in length by 3 in. (7.5 cm) wide. Each lasts for several days.

Caring for plants
Keep the compost moist, but never wet, in spring to autumn. In winter, apply only enough water to prevent the mix from drying out. Water with liquid tomato fertilizer once a month during spring to summer. Give the plant as much direct sun as possible all year to help it keep a good shape and encourage flowering.

Making more plants
Take offsets, if any are present, during summer, and allow it to dry for up to 3 days; then pot into cactus mix. If no offsets form, raise them from seed.

Parodia concinna

Parodia nivosa
No common name

6 in. (15 cm) high	2½ in. (6 cm) spread	Normal room temperature	Direct sunlight

This pretty little cactus originates from Argentina and grows as a spherical or short-cylindrical stem of dull green with a woolly white crown and 16–20 spirally arranged warty ribs. The round, white-felted areoles have white spines, with 15–20 around the outside and 3–5 longer spines in the center. In spring, vivid red, funnel-shaped flowers of up to 1¼ in. (3 cm) across are produced near the crown. This is an ideal plant for a sunny windowsill, although it may need protection from summer midday sun.

Caring for plants
Water moderately in spring to summer and allow to dry slightly between waterings. At all other times, water sparingly. Feed with standard liquid fertilizer once a month during spring and early summer.

Making more plants
Sow seed at 66–75°F (19–24°C) in spring.

Parodia nivosa

Passiflora 'Amethyst'
Passion flower

Up to 13 ft. (4 m) high

Cool room temperature

Direct sunlight (shade from midday summer sun)

This is a beautiful, vigorous climbing plant with smooth, slender stems and deeply 3-lobed leaves of a rich mid-green. In late summer and autumn, it produces wide-open amethyst purple flowers up to 4 in. (10 cm) across, with green anthers and sepals that reflex as the flower matures. The flowers are followed by egglike orange fruits up to 2½ in. (6 cm) long. This plant is hardy in many areas but makes a spectacular addition to the sunroom, cool greenhouse, or well-lit porch. The fruits are edible but full of seeds. Their flavor can be appreciated when strained into another fruit, such as apples.

Caring for plants
Water freely from spring until autumn; then apply only enough water to prevent the mix from drying out. Water with standard liquid fertilizer once a month during spring and early summer.

Making more plants
Take semiripe cuttings in summer, and root in a sterile mix.

Other varieties
Passiflora caerulea is a vigorous plant with deep green, angular stems, which climbs by using twisting tendrils. It flowers while still young, producing fat green buds along the stems, followed by 5 white sepals and 5 white petals of equal length, surrounding a circle of filaments shaded blue-purple, with a white band in the middle. *P. caerulea* 'Constance Elliott' has ivory-white flowers.

Top: *Passiflora* 'Amethyst'; Bottom: *Passiflora caerulea*

Pelargonium spp. Scented leaf Geranium

12–18 in. (30–45 cm) high | 12–18 in. (30–45 cm) spread | Normal room temperature | Indirect sunlight

A range of new scented-leaf geraniums has become available in recent years, lending fragrance as well as color to any display. The leaves are attractively cut or divided and are generally a matte mid-green, although varieties such as 'Lady Plymouth' are variegated. Use at the front of a display or on a pedestal or windowsill, where the foliage will be brushed past to release the scents of lemon, lime, mint, lilac, or rose. The variety 'Fragrans' has white flowers, and the foliage smells of nutmeg, apple, and pine. 'Attar of Roses' has lilac-pink flowers, and the leaves are scented with lemon and rose.

Caring for plants
Water moderately and allow to dry slightly between waterings. Water with standard liquid fertilizer at half strength every 2 weeks from spring to late summer.

Making more plants
Take tip or stem cuttings in spring or early summer, and remove small stipules and leaves from the lower third of the stem. Allow to wilt for 30 minutes before inserting into potting soil. Do not use rooting hormone on cuttings, because they naturally contain high levels of hormone and adding extra will make the stem rot.

Pelargonium Scented leaf

Pelargonium crispum
Lemon geranium

| Up to 24 in. (60 cm) high if left unchecked | Normal room temperature | Indirect sunlight |

This is a scented-leaf geranium that is grown for its aromatic foliage rather than its small pink flowers. The stems stand stiffly upright, although regular pinching can be used to control the overall shape of the plant. The rough-textured leaves are ½ in. (12 mm) across, rounded, and scented strongly of lemon. *Pelargonium crispum* 'Major' has larger leaves; in *P. crispum* 'Minor' the leaves are very small and crisped; *P. crispum* 'Peach Cream' has pink flowers with a peach scent; and *P. crispum* 'Variegatum' has leaves edged with creamy yellow.

Caring for plants
Water moderately and allow to dry slightly between waterings. Water with standard liquid fertilizer at half strength every 2 weeks from spring to late summer.

Making more plants
Take tip or stem cuttings in spring or early summer and remove small stipules and leaves from the lower third of the stem. Allow to wilt for 30 minutes before inserting into potting soil. Do not use rooting hormone on cuttings, because they naturally contain high levels of hormone and adding extra will make the stem rot.

Pelargonium crispum

Pelargonium x *domesticum*
Geranium

18 in.
(47 cm)
high

Normal
room
temperature

Indirect
sunlight

This is a large group of hybrids of complicated origins, with thick, branching stems and hairy, toothed leaves up to 4 in. (10 cm) across. The flowers are large and showy, borne in upright clusters, in single or combined shades of white, pink, salmon, orange, red, or purple. They are usually single, and the upper petals are often blotched with a darker color. *Pelargonium* 'Carisbrooke' has large pink flowers marked with wine red; *P.* 'Grand Slam' has rose-red flowers with darker markings; *P.* 'Pompeii' is a compact plant, which has nearly black petals with narrow pink-white edges.

Caring for plants
Water moderately and allow to dry slightly between waterings. Water with standard liquid fertilizer at half strength every 2 weeks from spring to late summer.

Making more plants
Take tip or stem cuttings in spring or early summer, and remove small stipules and leaves from the lower third of the stem. Allow to wilt for 30 minutes before inserting into potting soil. Do not use rooting hormone on cuttings, because they naturally contain high levels of hormone and adding extra will make the stem rot.

Pelargonium x *domesticum*

Pelargonium x *hortorum*
Fireworks series
Geranium

| 12–14 in. (30–35 cm) high | 12–14 in. (30–35 cm) spread | Normal room temperature | Indirect sunlight |

The name Fireworks relates to the unique starburst appearance of the flowers of this form, with their narrow, serrated petals. The foliage is a matte dark green, forming a neat, compact, low-growing mound. Flower colors include cherry, scarlet, salmon, light pink, and white. Two-tone flower colors include cherry and white, and red and white. These are attractive plants to use if space is limited because they are ideal as specimens. They enjoy higher temperatures and will quickly grow to fill a container, giving a colorful display throughout the season.

Caring for plants
Water moderately and allow to dry slightly between waterings. Water with standard liquid tomato fertilizer at half strength every 2 weeks from spring to late summer.

Making more plants
Take tip or stem cuttings in spring or early summer, and remove small stipules and leaves from the lower third of the stem. Allow to wilt for 30 minutes before inserting into potting soil. Do not use rooting hormone on cuttings, because they naturally contain high levels of hormone and adding extra will make the stem rot.

Other varieties
Pelargonium x *hortorum* 'Bull's Eye' has an amazing rich, dark, chocolate foliage, with a lime-green edge, making it particularly eye-catching as a specimen plant.

Top and Bottom: *Pelargonium x hortorum* Fireworks series

Pellaea rotundifolia
Button fern

4 in.
(10 cm)
high

18 in.
(47 cm)
spread

Normal
room
temperature

Indirect
sunlight,
partial shade

Unlike most ferns, pellaea prefers a dry environment rather than moist conditions. It has stout, creeping rhizomes giving rise to red-brown, scaly leaf stalks. The low, arching and spreading fronds are up to 12 in. (30 cm) long, and are a dull dark green. They have pairs of glossy pinnae that are round at first, becoming oval as they age, each minutely toothed. The outline of this plant makes it an ideal choice as a filler plant in a larger display, particularly at the front of an arrangement to hide the container and soften the outline.

Caring for plants
Keep the soil mix thoroughly moist all year round. Reduce watering if the temperature is low in winter; mist once a day if it rises in summer. Water with standard liquid fertilizer once a month during spring to autumn.

Making more plants
Divide mature plants in spring or grow from spores.

Pellaea rotundifolia

Pennisetum glaucum
'Purple Majesty'
No common name

| 60 in. (150 cm) high | (24 in.) (60 cm) spread | Normal room temperature | Direct sun for the best color |

This is an attractive annual grass, a form of ornamental millet, and it will add height and color to any mixed planting display. Its exotic-looking, glossy foliage starts off mid-green, then develops a purple midrib, and gradually turns a dark reddish purple. The central flower spike can be up to 18 in. (47 cm) long and is covered with golden pollen until the seed sets. Afterward it can be left as an unusual spiky feature until the plant dies down, when it can be dried for use in indoor flower arrangements or left outside for wild birds to eat.

Caring for plants
Keep the soil mix moist but not wet. Water with standard liquid fertilizer every 2 weeks during spring and early summer.

Making more plants
As an F1 plant, this will not produce seed that grows true to type, so seed must be purchased for reliable results.

Top and Bottom: *Pennisetum glaucum* 'Purple Majesty'

Pentas lanceolata
Egyptian star cluster

18 in.
(47 cm)
high

Normal room
temperature,
minimum
50°F (10°C)

Direct
sunlight

This is an attractive and unusual soft-wooded shrub with 4-in. (10-cm)-long, hairy, lance-shaped leaves. The flowers are borne in 4-in. (10-cm)-clusters. Each individual, tubular bloom opens out in a 5-pointed star shape, measuring ½ in. (12 mm) across, usually in autumn and winter but also at other times. The flowers can be in shades of magenta, red, mauve, pink or white, according to the variety.

Caring for plants
Keep moist throughout the year except for a 6–8 week period immediately after flowering, when only sufficient water should be applied to prevent the mix from drying out. Water with standard liquid fertilizer once a month all year except during the rest period. Pinching out the shoot tips regularly will produce a bushy plant.

Making more plants
Take 3–4-in. (7.5–10-cm)-long tip cuttings from nonflowering shoots in spring or summer.

Pentas lanceolata

Peperomia caperata
Emerald-ripple pepper

8 in.
(20 cm)

Normal
room
temperature

Indirect
sunlight

This is a small plant with heart-shaped, glossy, emerald green, deeply rippled leaves up to 1¼ in. (3 cm) long. At the bottom of the ridges, the leaf looks almost black. The leaf petioles are green to dull red and up to 3 in. (7.5 cm) long. *Peperomia caperata* 'Emerald Ripple' is a more compact plant with smaller leaves, *P. caperata* 'Little Fantasy' is a dwarf form.

Caring for plants
Keep the soil mix barely moist at all times. High humidity is important, but if the pot is standing on a tray of moist pebbles, make sure that the plant is set high and cannot take up the extra water. Water with half-strength liquid fertilizer once a month in spring to autumn.

Making more plants
Take leaf cuttings in spring or summer. Use the whole leaf with 1 in. (2.5 cm) of stalk attached, and insert it until the edge of the leaf is in contact with the rooting medium.

Peperomia caperata

Peperomia glabella
Radiator plant

8 in.
(20 cm)
high

Normal
room
temperature

Indirect
sunlight

This is an erect or sprawling plant, with soft fleshy, glossy red stems and mid-green, oval, fleshy leaves, on ½ in. (12-mm)-red petioles. The thin, green-white flower stalks reach up to 6 in. (15 cm) high. This is an attractive plant to use as a foil to brighter colors within a mixed arrangement. *Peperomia glabella*. 'Variegata' has pale green leaves, edged or variegated off-white.

Caring for plants
Keep the soil mix barely moist at all times. High humidity is important, but if the pot is standing on a tray of moist pebbles, make sure that the plant is set high and cannot take up the extra water. Water with half-strength liquid fertilizer once a month from spring to autumn.

Making more plants
Take 3-in. (7.5-cm)-long tip cuttings in spring or summer, and root them in a sterile medium.

Peperomia glabella

Peperomia obtusifolia
Baby rubber plant, American rubber plant, Pepper-face

| 12 in. (30 cm) high | Normal room temperature | Indirect sunlight |

Peperomia obtusifolia is stoloniferous, sending up purplish stems and rooting as it spreads. The rounded fleshy leaves are a deep purple-green color, and short white flower stalks are produced during spring and autumn. *P. obtusifolia* 'Alba' is a form with cream new growth and spotted red stems and petioles. *P. obtusifolia* 'Albo-marginata' has small gray-green leaves edged in cream. *P. obtusifolia* 'Minima' is a dwarf form, with glossy and densely packed leaves. *P. obtusifolia* 'Variegata' has pointed leaves with cream markings on pale green and scarlet stems.

Caring for plants
Keep the soil mix barely moist at all times. Water with half-strength liquid fertilizer once a month from spring to autumn. High humidity is important, but if the pot is standing on a tray of moist pebbles, make sure that the plant is high and cannot take up the extra water.

Making more plants
Take 3-in. (7.5-cm)-long tip cuttings in spring or summer, and root them in a sterile medium.

Peperomia obtusifolia

Pericallis x *hybrida* (was *Cineraria cruenta*)
Florist's cineraria

Up to 18 in.
(47 cm)
high

Cool room
temperature

Indirect
sunlight,
cool light

Although this is actually a perennial plant, it is usually grown as an annual to be discarded after flowering. The large, dome-shaped cluster of daisylike flowers is set within a circle of hairy, heart-shaped, mid-green leaves and can be white, pink, terra-cotta, red, maroon, purple, violet, or blue, according to the variety, often with a white base to the petals. Many different flower forms are available, with single, double, or star-shaped flowers in either large or more compact forms. For the maximum flowering period, buy a plant with only a few open flowers—to show the color—and plenty of buds.

Caring for plants
Keep the soil mix thoroughly moist, but do not allow the plant to stand in water. Fertilizing is unnecessary for the period the plant is indoors.

Making more plants
Sow seed in late spring or summer, but raising new plants is not easy.

Pericallis x *hybrida*

Petroselinum crispum
Parsley

12 in.
(30 cm)
high

Normal
room
temperature

Indirect
sunlight

This is a hardy biennial herb that grows well in pots. It has crinkled, bright green leaves that can be used as a garnish and in sauces, fish, and egg dishes. The leaves should be used fresh in the first year—although they can be dried or frozen, they lose much of their taste. Once the plant flowers, the leaves become rather bitter. Grow on a kitchen windowsill for a fresh supply all year round.

Caring for plants
Keep the soil mix moist at all times, but there is no need to fertilize. By removing the flower heads, the quality and usable life of the foliage are improved.

Making more plants
Sow seed in a rich potting soil. Germination can take 6–8 weeks, but can be hastened by soaking the seed overnight and by trickling a little boiling water over it immediately after planting.

Petroselinum crispum

Phalaenopsis amabilis
Moth orchid

12–36 in. (30–90 cm) high	10–12 in. (25–30 cm) spread	Normal room temperature. During winter rest period, keep at about 60°F (15°C).	Indirect sunlight

This variety of *Phalaenopsis* has pure white flowers with central "lips" of yellow streaked with deep pink. The flowers are borne on single or branched stems that arise from the base of the leaves, and the flowering stem may last for many months with the flowers opening successively. They are often produced throughout the year if conditions are suitable. The flowers of *P. amabilis* are not scented.

Caring for plants
From spring to autumn, water and mist daily. In winter, water sparingly and stop misting. Water with standard liquid fertilizer once a month. Grow in fine-grade epiphytic orchid medium in a slatted basket to allow aerial roots to hang outside.

Making more plants
Take offshoots when the plant fills the pot, and plant in fine-grade epiphytic orchid medium.

Other varieties
Phalaenopsis 'Brother Sara Gold' has wide yellow-orange petals streaked and spotted with darker pink and central "lips" of deep pink. The flowers are scented and often produced throughout the year if conditions are suitable.

Phalaenopsis amabilis

Philodendron bipinnatifidum (syn. *P. selloum*)
Tree philodendron

Up to 15 ft. (5 m) high   Normal room temperature   Indirect sunlight, partial shade

This is a treelike shrub, usually with a single, sturdy, upright stem that is inclined to fall over and lie horizontally as it ages, with just the tip pointing upward. The downward-pointing leaves grow to 39 in. (100 cm) long, half of which is the petiole. They are heart-shaped, bright green, and deeply cut, with many narrow, wavy-edged lobes. The flower is a spathe 12 in. (30 cm) long and cream with a red margin. *Philodendron bipinnatifidum* 'German Selloum' is a form with finely cut leaves and wavy, graceful lobes, *P. bipinnatifidum* 'Miniature Selloum' is a dwarf form, with small leaves and thick petioles; *P. bipinnatifidum* 'Variegatum' has leaves blotched light green to yellow.

Caring for plants
Keep moist from spring to autumn. In winter, apply only sufficient water to prevent the mix from drying out. Water with standard liquid fertilizer once a month in spring to summer. Variegated plants always need more light than green forms; the plant will compensate for the low light by converting the yellow leaf areas to green, and the markings will fade or be lost altogether.

Making more plants
Sow fresh seed in spring, or take tip cuttings taken from shoots at the base of the plant.

Philodendron bipinnatifidum (syn. *P. selloum*)

Philodendron 'Emerald Queen'
Philodendron

Up to 10 ft.
(3 m) high

Normal
room
temperature

Indirect
sunlight
or partial
shade

This is a vigorous hybrid of unknown origins, ideal for growing on a moss pole because the foliage is a uniform size. The glossy, bright green leaves are medium-sized, arrow-shaped, on short petioles, and closely spaced along the stems. This is a plant grown particularly for its resistance to both cold and disease. Once the roots attach themselves to a moss pole, the plant should become self-supporting, with no need for unsightly ties or string.

Caring for plants
Keep moist in spring to autumn. In winter, apply only sufficient water to prevent the medium from drying out. For the aerial roots to cling to the moss pole, it should be kept moist at all times. Water with standard liquid fertilizer once a month during spring to summer.

Making more plants
Take 4-in. (10-cm)-long tip cuttings in spring or summer, and root in a sterile medium.

Philodendron 'Emerald Queen'

Phoenix canariensis
Canary date palm

72 in.
(180 cm)
high

Normal room
temperature,
with a winter
rest period at
50–55°F (10–12°C)

Direct
sunlight

This is a decorative palm, with a single, bulbous stem marked with oblong leaf scars. The fronds are emerald green and arch gracefully, with stiff pinnae arranged along a lighter green midrib. This is one of the hardiest palms, because it is tolerant of temperature variations and direct sunlight, and not easily damaged. It is slow-growing, reaching only about 72 in. (180 cm) with fronds up to 36 in. (90 cm) long, making it a good plant to use as a specimen in a greenhouse.

Caring for plants
Keep thoroughly moist in spring through autumn. In winter, apply only sufficient water to prevent the mix from drying out. Avoid overwatering and never allow the pot to stand in water or the roots will rot. Water with standard liquid fertilizer once a month during spring to summer.

Making more plants
Sow seed in a germinating soil mix, and keep it at around 80°F (25°C).

Phoenix canariensis

Pilea cadierei
Aluminium plant

18 in.
(47 cm)
high

Warm,
minimum
55°F (12°C)

Indirect
sunlight,
partial shade

This is an easily grown, upright plant, with unusual, metallic silver markings on the leaves. The slender branchlets are green tinted pink, but they are inclined to become bare at the base and straggly as the plant ages. The leaves are oval in shape, toothed around the edges, and marked with silver on a dark green background—sometimes to the extent that the whole leaf appears a metallic silver color. The markings are caused by tiny pockets of air within the leaf, between the veins, raising the surface slightly and producing an opalescent effect. *Pilea cadierei* 'Minima' is a dwarf form, densely branched with pink stems, and scalloped leaves that are deep olive green with raised silver patches.

Caring for plants
Keep the soil mix barely moist at all times. Water with half-strength liquid fertilizer every 2 weeks in spring to summer. Regular pinching the growing tips will encourage a bushy plant that will not become straggly as quickly.

Making more plants
Take 3-in. (7.5-cm)-long tip cuttings in spring or summer, and root in a sterile medium.

Pilea cadierei

Pleione bulbocodioides
Indian crocus

6 in.
(15 cm)
high

12 in.
(30 cm)
spread

Cool room
temperature

Indirect
sunlight

These attractive terrestrial orchids have rounded pseudobulbs and narrow, folded, dull to mid-green, straplike leaves that grow up to 6 in. (15 cm) long. Each pseudobulb will produce a single narcissus-like flower during the spring, which is lilac-pink in color with pale pink margins on the petals and pinkish brown mottled markings inside the center. Each flower is around 3 in. (7.5 cm) across and carried on short greenish brown stems up to 4 in. (10 cm) long.

Caring for plants
Water freely in spring and summer. Water with standard liquid fertilizer once a month during summer.

Making more plants
Divide and repot in early spring. Always divide annually and discard old pseudobulbs.

Pleione bulbocodioides

Plumbago auriculata
Cape leadwort

Up to 10 ft. (3 m) high	Normal room temperature. Winter rest period should be at 45–50°F (7–10°C).	Direct sunlight

This is an evergreen shrub, with long, arching stems that need to be tied to supports to prevent them from straggling. Pretty sky blue flowers are borne in clusters of up to 20 throughout spring, summer, and autumn amid long oval, mid-green leaves. The individual flowers are tubular, flaring out into 5 petals, each of which is marked with a darker blue central stripe. *Plumbago auriculata alba* is a form with pure white flowers.

Caring for plants

Keep thoroughly moist in spring to autumn. In winter, apply only sufficient water to prevent the soil mix drying out. Fertilize with a high-potash fertilizer, such as tomato fertilizer, every 2 weeks from spring to summer. Remove flowers as they fade to promote the production of more buds. Flowers are produced on the current season's growth, so any pruning should be done in early spring to give the maximum flowering time. When pruning, reduce growth by up to two-thirds.

Making more plants

Take 3–4-in. (7.5–10-cm)-long cuttings in spring or summer, air layer stem, or sow seed.

Plumbago auriculata

Plumeria rubra
Frangipani

| 72 in. (180 cm) high | 36 in. (90 cm) spread | Normal room temperature | Direct sunlight |

In its natural habitat, this plant would grow to become a large deciduous shrub or small tree, but indoors, where its size will be restricted, it is a wonderful, heavily scented addition to a mixed collection of container plants. It has an upright habit, with alternately arranged, long oval, glossy green leaves up to 12 in. (30 cm) long. The impressively fragrant flowers are produced at the tips of the shoots during summer and autumn. Each wide-open bloom has slightly overlapping petals with a yellow eye and measures up to 4 in. (10 cm) across. Shades vary to include red, rose-pink, yellow, and bronze. The milky sap can be an irritant and should be avoided.

Caring for plants
Keep moist from spring to autumn. In winter, apply sufficient water to prevent the soil mix from drying out. Water with standard liquid fertilizer monthly during spring to late summer.

Making more plants
Take cuttings of bare stems in spring and allow the base to dry before inserting into a sterile medium.

Top and Bottom: *Plumeria rubra*

Polyscias guilfoylei
Geranium aralia, Wild coffee

Up to 10 ft.
(3 m) high

Warm,
minimum
65°F (18°C)

Indirect
sunlight

This is an evergreen shrub or small tree with upright, sparsely branched stems, usually bearing its attractive foliage only at the tips. The leaves are 12–18 in. (30–47 cm) long, divided into 5–9 leaflets, each mid-green with a creamy white margin and deeply toothed. This plant is ideal for a warm greenhouse, but may be too large to use as a houseplant. One of its forms would then be more appropriate. *Polyscias guilfoylei* 'Crispa' is compact, with sharply toothed, bronze-tinted leaves; *P. guilfoylei* 'Laciniata' has doubly pinnate, drooping leaves, with white toothed margins; *P. guilfoylei* 'Victoriae' (Lace aralia) is compact and grows to 36 in. (90 cm), with finely dissected leaves, each leaflet having a pure white margin.

Caring for plants
Keep the soil mix moist throughout the year. Increase humidity by setting the pot on a tray of moist pebbles. Polyscias do not have a definite rest period—the growth will just slow down during the winter months—so it is essential to maintain a moist soil mix. Water with standard liquid fertilizer every 2 weeks from spring to autumn.

Making more plants
Take 4-in. (10-cm)-long tip cuttings in spring, and root in a sterile medium.

Polyscias guilfoylei

Polystichum tsussimense
Holly fern, Korean rock fern

| 16 in. (40cm) high | 16 in. (40 cm) spread | 60–70°F (15–20°C) | Indirect sunlight |

This is an evergreen fern from northeast Asia that grows into a shuttlecock-shaped plant, with broad, dark green fronds. Each frond is lance-shaped, with spiny-toothed and pointed pinnae. Ferns cannot thrive if they are neglected. They need both moist air and potting soil, while dry air, gas fumes, and cold drafts will harm them, as well as allowing the soil mix to dry out and then soaking it.

Caring for plants

Keep moist, but do not allow it to become water-logged. This plant will benefit from monthly fertilizing throughout the growing season. Remove older fronds as their appearance deteriorates—a few at a time from right at their base in spring each year—to allow space for new shoots to develop.

Making more plants

Divide mature plants in spring, or break off new clumps from the rhizome with 1 or 2 fronds attached.

Polystichum tsussimense

Portulaca grandiflora
Purslane

12–14 in.
(30–35 cm)
high

24 in.
(60 cm)
spread

Normal
room
temperature

Direct sunlight
(avoid midday
summer sun
behind glass)

Purslane is a semisucculent plant, grown for its showy, cup-shaped blooms in white and shades of yellow, apricot, pink, red, and purple. The plant may be mound-forming or trailing and thrives in a container in a hot, sunny position. New introductions include the Fairytales series, including 'Cinderella', which has double flowers with a bright pink center and yellow outer petals; 'Sleeping Beauty', with double, bright golden-yellow flowers; and 'Snow White', which has double flowers with crisp, pure-white petals. These have a low, spreading growth habit and are both heat and drought tolerant. They are ideal to trail from a pedestal or windowsill, and the bright colors make them attractive as specimen plants.

Caring for plants
Keep the soil mix moist, but allow it to dry slightly between waterings. Water with standard liquid tomato fertilizer at half strength every 2 weeks during spring and summer.

Making more plants
This plant needs to be purchased as a young plant in spring. It is best treated as an annual and replaced each year.

Portulaca grandiflora

Primula obconica
German primrose,
Poison primrose

| 12 in. (30 cm) high | Cool, 50–55°F (10–12°C) | Cool light |

This is a pretty plant for indoors; it produces masses of large, fragrant blooms during the early months of the year in shades of white, pink, salmon, lilac, magenta, or red, each with a distinctive apple green eye. They can be grouped together for instant effect or used to add short-term color to a more permanent foliage arrangement. The flowers are borne in clusters on 12 in. (30 cm) stalks emerging from leaves that are roughly circular in shape, coarse in texture, and covered with fine hairs. *The fine hairs that cover the leaves may cause skin irritation.*

Caring for plants
Keep the soil mix thoroughly moist. Water with standard liquid fertilizer every 2 weeks. Picking off the flowers as they fade will prolong the flowering period. *Primula obconica* is usually treated as an annual and discarded after flowering, but it can be brought back for a second year by keeping it cool and barely moist after flowering until autumn, when it can be repotted and the watering increased.

Making more plants
Sow seed in spring, but it is not easy to get new plants to grow.

Primula obconica

Primula Pruhonicensis hybrids
Polyanthus

Up to 8 in. (20 cm) high

Cool, 50–55°F (10–12°C)

Cool light

This name covers a vast number of hybrids produced by interbreeding several species, including *Primula elatior, P. juliae, P. veris,* and *P. vulgaris.* They may be primrose-type with single flowers on short stalks, or cow-/ox-lip type with clusters of flowers on longer, stout, hairy stalks. All have a rosette of oval, heavily veined mid-green leaves, and the flowers are produced in shades of white, yellow, pink, orange, red, or blue, usually with a yellow eye, in late winter and spring. They can be placed individually, grouped together for a splash of color, or used to add short-term color to a more permanent foliage arrangement. Unlike some of the tender indoor primulas, the polyanthus group can be planted outdoors when flowering has finished as they are frost-hardy and will continue flowering for many years. Choose a lightly shaded position and keep well watered until they are established.

Caring for plants
Keep the potting soil thoroughly moist. Water with standard liquid fertilizer every 2 weeks.

Making more plants
Sow seed in a fine germinating mix in summer.

Primula Pruhonicensis Hybrids

Protea eximia
Protea

| 8 ft. (2.5 m) high | 5 ft. (1.5 m) spread | Cool room temperature | Direct sunlight |

This broadly columnar, shrubby plant originates from South Africa. It has reddish green stems that turn brown with age and are clad with broadly oval leaves about 4 in. (10 cm) long. They are tinged purple when young, later turning silvery green and with a felty covering over the surface. During spring and summer, shuttlecock-shaped flower heads, up to 6 in. (15 cm) across, are produced on the shoot tips. The flower bracts have red or reddish pink tints and are fringed with white hairs.

Caring for plants
Water moderately from spring until autumn; then apply only enough water to prevent the mix from drying out. This plant needs a neutral to acidic soil mix. Water with standard liquid fertilizer at half strength once a month during spring and autumn.

Making more plants
Take semiripe cuttings in summer and root in a sterile medium, making sure it is neutral to acidic.

Top and Bottom: *Protea eximia*

Pteris cretica
Table fern, Cretan brake

12 in.
(30 cm)
high

Normal room
temperature
all year round

Indirect
sunlight
or warm
partial
shade (not
deep shade)

This is a neat, small fern that forms a clump of fronds from a short underground rhizome. Each frond has a slender stalk of 8–10 in. (20–25 cm) long, and arching pinnae, which can be striped, variegated, or plain, according to the variety, and carried singly or in forked pairs. *Pteris cretica albolineata* has leaf segments with a broad white stripe; *P. cretica* 'Parkeri' is a larger plant, with glossy fronds and finely toothed leaflets. *P. cretica* 'Rivertoniana' has deeply lobed leaves and pinnae in 4–5 pairs.

Caring for plants
Keep the soil mix thoroughly moist at all times. In higher temperatures, increase the humidity by setting the pot on a tray of moist pebbles. Water with half-strength liquid fertilizer once a month in spring to autumn. Cut out older fronds as they fade to make room for new ones.

Making more plants
Divide larger plants in spring or propagate from spores.

Pteris cretica

Radermachera sinica
No common name

39 in.
(100 cm)
high

Normal
room
temperature

Indirect
sunlight

This is a relatively new entry to the indoor plant selection, having been introduced in the early 1980s from Taiwan. It owes its popularity to its tolerance to dry, centrally heated air. It is an evergreen shrub with large, graceful, compound leaves up to 30 in. (75 cm) long and glossy, deeply veined leaflets. The fragrant, deep yellow flowers are produced only on mature plants. This is an ideal plant for a softening effect in a large arrangement and for framing flowering plants.

Caring for plants
Keep the soil mix moist at all times. Do not allow it to become waterlogged or dry out, both of which will cause the lower leaves to drop prematurely. Water with standard liquid fertilizer every 2 weeks during spring to autumn.

Making more plants
Take 4-in. (10-cm)-long tip cuttings in spring or summer, and root in a sterile medium.

Radermachera sinica

Rebutia minuscula
Red crown cactus

6 in. (15 cm) high	6 in. (15 cm) spread in 4 years	Normal room temperature. Winter min. 40°F (5°C)	Direct sunlight (shade from midday in summer sun)

This is a small but quick-growing desert cactus that easily produces offsets from the base and flowers while still young. Each individual stem is globular in shape, reaching up to 2 in. (5 cm) in diameter, and covered in tubercles arranged in 16–20 spiral ridges. The thin, white bristly spines are 1¼ in. (3 cm) long, in clusters of around 20. Pale red flowers appear in late spring around the base of the stems, each lasting 2–3 days, over a period of several weeks.

Caring for plants
Keep moist from spring to autumn. In winter, apply sufficient water to prevent the soil mix from drying out. Water with standard liquid fertilizer at half strength once a month during spring and early summer.

Making more plants
Offsets can be cut or pulled gently from the plant and potted in a cactus soil mix. Grows readily from seed, often flowering at the end of the first growing season. This plant can literally flower itself to death in 5–6 years, so it is wise to propagate a particular favorite from offsets before this happens.

Rebutia minuscula

Rebutia senilis
Red crown cactus

| 4 in. (10 cm) high | 6 in. (15 cm) spread in 4 years | Normal room temperature. Winter min. 40°F (5°C) | Direct sunlight (shade from midday summer sun) |

This small but quick-growing genus of cactus from Argentina easily produces offsets from the base and flowers while still quite young. The individual stems are globe-shaped and are covered in tubercles arranged in ridges with bristly, thin white spines, 1¼ in. (3 cm) long, in clusters of around 20. Pale red flowers appear in late spring around the base of the stems, giving rise to the plant's common name. They are borne over a period of several weeks, and each lasts 2–3 days.

Caring for plants
Keep moist from spring to autumn. In winter, apply sufficient water to prevent the soil mix from drying out. Water with standard liquid fertilizer at half strength once a month during spring and early summer.

Making more plants
Offsets can be cut or pulled gently from the plant and potted in cactus compost. Grows readily from seed, often flowering at the end of the first growing season. This plant can literally flower itself to death in 5–6 years, so it is wise to propagate a particular favorite from offsets before this happens.

Rebutia senilis

Rhapis excelsa
Lady palm, Ground rattan, Bamboo palm

60 in.
(150 cm)
high

Normal room
temperature or
cooler. Minimum
45°F (7°C)

Indirect sunlight,
cool light. Direct
sunlight in
winter

This is a graceful, slow-growing palm that looks spectacular as an individual specimen as it ages. The leaf petiole is equal in length to the blade, which is dark green and divided up to 10 times to within a few centimeters of the rachis, giving it a fanlike appearance. The leaves are borne on reedlike stems, which are clothed with coarse brown fibers. As the lower leaves age and fall off, they take some of the fiber with them, leaving scars on the previously smooth stem. *Rhapis excelsa* 'Variegata' has palmate, leathery leaves with segments striped white, while *R. excelsa* 'Zuikonishiki' has leaves with yellow-edged segments.

Caring for plants
Keep the soil mix moist during spring to autumn, but drier in winter. Avoid overwatering, and never allow the pot to stand in water, or the roots will rot. Water with standard liquid fertilizer once a month in spring to summer.

Making more plants
Detach basal suckers in spring or summer, and pot in a free-draining potting soil.

Top and Bottom: *Rhapis excelsa*

Rhododendron simsii (*Azalea indica*)
Indian azalea

12–18 in.
(30–47 cm)
high

Cool, 45-60°F
(7-15°C)

Cool light

This is the florist's azalea, which is found in large quantities and a wide range of colors throughout winter and spring each year. It gives a spectacular display, with a succession of flowers over a period of about 6 weeks in shades of white, pink, red, purple, or a combination. Each individual bloom lasts several days and should be removed as it fades to ensure continued production. Buy a plant with only a few open blooms—to ascertain the color—and plenty of buds, because this will ensure the maximum display.

Caring for plants
This plant needs to be kept wet, not just moist, in order to thrive. They are acid-loving plants and may begin to suffer if they are watered with hard tap water. Using rainwater will help if the leaves begin to turn yellow (chlorosis). Repot into an ericaceous soil mix once flowering is over. Water with standard liquid fertilizer every 2 weeks in spring to summer, then once a month in autumn. Remove only the petals of the faded flowers when deadheading. The new shoots that follow the flowers arise from the same point on the stem, so cutting off the whole flower head will remove the shoot buds, too.

Making more plants
Take 2-in. (5-cm)-long tip cuttings in late spring from the new growth. Use rooting hormone and pot in an ericaceous potting mix.

Rhododendron simsii (*Azalea indica*)

Rosa chinensis 'Minima'
Fairy rose

Up to 12 in.
(30 cm)
high

Normal room
temperature

Direct
sunlight

There is a tendency to view roses as outdoor plants, but the miniature varieties make excellent indoor flowering specimens, giving color and fragrance throughout the summer. The flowers can be single, semidouble, or fully double, with colors that include red, pink, yellow, white, and a range of shades in between. After flowering, they can be planted in the garden or, with a little attention, kept for future use indoors.

Caring for plants
Keep the soil mix moist during spring to autumn. High humidity is important, so stand the pot on a tray of moist pebbles. In winter, apply only sufficient water to prevent the mix from drying out. Water with standard liquid fertilizer every 2 weeks in spring to summer. If the plant is to be kept, it will need a winter rest period of 8 weeks at 45°F (7°C) or lower. To bring the plant back into flower indoors a second year, repot in autumn and set the plant outside. Bring indoors in January, acclimatizing gradually if possible, rather than putting it straight into a warm room. Prune to outward-facing buds to shorten each stem by half, increase watering and feeding, and the plant could be in flower by early spring.

Making more plants
Take 2-in. (5-cm)-long tip cuttings in spring, use a rooting hormone, and root in a sterile medium.

Rosa chinensis 'Minima'

Ruellia makoyana
Monkey plant,
Trailing velvet plant

Stems to
24 in.
(60 cm)
long

Warm,
55°F (12°C)
minimum

Indirect
sunlight

This is a spreading plant, with weak stems up to 24 in. (60 cm) long, that can trail gracefully from a hanging basket or be tied to a support and pinched on a regular basis to encourage bushiness. The pointed oval leaves are velvety to the touch, olive green tinted violet above, purple beneath, and veined in silvery gray. Masses of single, trumpet-shaped, rosy carmine flowers up to 2 in. (5 cm) across are produced in winter and early spring.

Caring for plants
Keep the soil mix moist throughout the year except during the 6-week rest period immediately after flowering when only sufficient water should be applied to prevent it from drying out. High humidity is essential, so set the pot on a tray of moist pebbles. Water with standard liquid fertilizer every 2 weeks except during the rest period.

Making more plants
Take 3–4-in. (7.5–10-cm)-tip cuttings in summer, and root in a sterile medium.

Ruellia makoyana

Saintpaulia ionantha (*Saintpaulia velutina*)
African violet

4 in. (10 cm) high	6 in. (15 cm) spread	Normal room temperature. Protect from drafts and sudden temperature changes.	Indirect sunlight

An ever popular indoor plant due both to its compact size, which is small enough to fit comfortably on a windowsill, and its long flowering period. The velvety leaves are up to 1½ in. (4 cm) across, slightly scalloped around the edge, with erect hairs on the upper surface, and colored red-maroon beneath. Clusters of flowers are produced on upright stalks of up to 2 in. (5 cm) long, in shades of purple, violet, blue, mauve, and white.

Caring for plants
Keep the soil mix moist, but not wet, or the roots will rot. The leaves and flowers are easily damaged by water falling on them, so always water from below and never mist. Increase the humidity by setting the pot on a tray of moist pebbles instead. Water with standard liquid fertilizer every 2 weeks during spring to autumn. Saintpaulias grow best when they are in plastic pots and are slightly pot-bound.

Making more plants
Take whole leaf petiole cuttings, and root in a sterile medium.

Saintpaulia ionantha (Saintpaulia velutina)

Sansevieria trifasciata
Mother-in-law's tongue, Snake plant

24 in. (60 cm) high

Normal room temperature, minimum 55°F (12°C)

Tolerant of direct sunlight, indirect sunlight, and shade

This is one plant that seems to survive where no others can. It is tolerant of sunshine and shade, dry air, drafts, and even a certain amount of neglect in terms of watering. Each rhizomatous plant can last many years, because the rate of growth is slow, and they seldom need repotting. The leaves are narrow, flat, long, and pointed, held stiffly erect and banded light and dark green. *Sansevieria trifasciata* 'Laurentii' is a form in which the leaf margins are bright yellow, while *S. trifasciata* 'Golden Hahnii' has leaves that form a squat rosette and are banded gray with cream margins.

Caring for plants
Keep the soil mix moist during spring to autumn. In winter, apply only sufficient water to prevent the compost from drying out. Water with half-strength liquid fertilizer once a month in spring to summer. Sansevierias grow best when slightly pot-bound, so do not repot each year.

Making more plants
Divide clumps of the mature plant so that each new piece has both leaves and roots, or take leaf cuttings by clipping 1 leaf into short pieces and inserting them base-downward into a pot or tray of potting soil. Because the yellow part of the variegated leaf contains no chlorophyll and cannot produce roots, plants propagated by leaf cuttings will be only green.

Sansevieria trifasciata

Saxifraga stolonifera
Mother of thousands,
Strawberry geranium

8 in.
(20 cm)
high

Cool

Indirect
sunlight,
partial shade

This is a small evergreen plant that spreads by means of long, thin, red stolons, which bear plantlets at their tips. The common name "Mother of thousands" arises from the copious quantities of these small plants that are produced. The round, bristly, long-stalked leaves are rosette or tuft forming, mid-green with silvery veins above and flushed red beneath. Branched flowering stems up to 15 in. (40 cm) long are produced in late summer and early autumn, bearing clusters of white flowers. *Saxifraga stolonifera* 'Tricolor' is less vigorous and has leaves edged cream with a pink flush. It needs a normal room temperature, rather than cool, with direct sunlight for at least part of each day to ensure good coloration.

Caring for plants
Keep the soil mix thoroughly moist in spring to autumn. In winter, apply only sufficient water to prevent the mix from drying out. In higher temperatures, increase the humidity using a tray of moist pebbles, but do not allow to stand in water or the roots will rot. Water with standard liquid fertilizer once a month during spring to summer.

Making more plants
Root the plantlets into small pots of potting soil, either before or after detaching from the parent plant.

Saxifraga stolonifera

Schefflera actinophylla
Umbrella tree

84 in.
(210 cm)
high

Normal
room
temperature

Indirect
sunlight

In its native habitat, this plant can become a tree up to 40 ft. (12 m) high, but indoors, it is more usual to see it as a pretty, bushy shrub, with leaves borne in terminal rosettes resembling the spokes of an umbrella, hence, the common name. The upright petioles can reach as long as 33 in. (80 cm), each bearing 7–16 glossy, bright green leaflets that grow to 12 x 4 in. (30 x 10 cm). Schefflera will look equally attractive grown as individual specimens or used in a group display, where the lush foliage softens outlines and acts as a foil for brighter-colored leaves or flowers.

Caring for plants
Keep the soil mix moist in spring to autumn. In winter, apply only sufficient water to prevent the mix from drying out. Increase humidity by setting the pot on a tray of moist pebbles and misting when temperatures are high. Water with standard liquid fertilizer once a month during spring to autumn.

Making more plants
Take tip cuttings in summer, use rooting hormone and seal in a plastic bag at 70°F (21°C).

Schefflera actinophylla

Schefflera elegantissima (Dizygotheca elegantissima)
False aralia, Finger aralia

39 in.
(100 cm)
high

Normal
room
temperature

Indirect
sunlight

This is one of the most graceful and delicate plants available for indoors. It is an elegant specimen with lacy, coppery green foliage. Each leaf comprises 7–10 narrow, toothed leaflets borne at the end of slim 4-in. (10-cm)-petioles. Both the stems and leaf petioles are mottled with white. It is attractive grown as a single specimen, and several plants can be grouped together in one pot to achieve a really bushy effect. It is also useful in a mixed arrangement where it can soften, fill gaps, and add an interesting color contrast.

Caring for plants
Keep moist in spring to autumn, but in winter, apply only sufficient water to prevent the mix from drying out. Increase humidity by setting the pot in a tray of moist pebbles, but keep the pot above water level. Water with standard liquid fertilizer every 2 weeks during spring to summer. Pinch regularly to achieve a bushy effect.

Making more plants
This is very difficult, but young plants are easily available to buy.

Schefflera elegantissima (Dizygotheca elegantissima)

Schizanthus
Poor man's orchid, Butterfly flower

| 12–18 in. (30–47 cm) high | 12 in. (30 cm) spread | Normal room temperature | Indirect sunlight |

A pretty annual with finely cut, almost ferny foliage on upright stems. Schizanthus can be raised very easily from seed and quickly produces a stunning display of two-lipped, orchidlike flowers in spikes on upright stems from spring until autumn. Flower colors include white and shades of yellow, amber, pink, red, and purple, with yellow throats, and many are flecked with contrasting colors. The flowers are up to 3 in. (7.5 cm) across. These form a dramatic massed display but are equally attractive used as single-specimen plants.

Caring for plants
Keep the soil mix moist at all times. Water with standard liquid tomato fertilizer at half strength every 2 weeks during spring and summer.

Making more plants
Sow seed in spring; then prick out into individual pots. Save any unused seed in a dark, airtight container for future use.

Top and Bottom: *Schizanthus*

Schlumbergera x *buckleyi*
Christmas cactus

12–18 in.
(30–47 cm)
spread in
10 years

Normal
room
temperature

Indirect
sunlight

There are more than 200 named cultivars of the "Christmas cactus," all of which flower during winter in shades of purple, pink, white, red, orange, or yellow. The arching stems are made of oblong, flattened segments, the edges of which are scalloped or toothed, with tiny areoles set both in the notches along the edges and at the end of each segment. The tip areoles are slightly elongated, and it is from these that the flowers develop singly or in pairs.

Caring for plants
Keep the soil mix moist at all times except for a 3–4-week rest period after flowering, when the mix should only be given enough water to prevent it from drying out. Feed with standard liquid tomato fertilizer every 2 weeks from the appearance of the flower buds until the last bud has opened. Stop fertilizing during the rest period; then apply standard liquid fertilizer once a month during the rest of the year. The buds are likely to drop off this plant if it is moved, subjected to a sudden change in temperature, or either over- or underwatered once they have started to form. During the summer (June–August), the plant may be placed in a shady spot outdoors, but it must be back inside before there is a risk of frost.

Making more plants
Take at least 2 segments by breaking them carefully from the parent plant. Push deeply enough into a small pot of soil mix to stand upright; then water gently to settle the mix. Several cuttings can be inserted into a larger pot for an immediate effect.

Schlumbergera x buckleyi

Scindapsus pictus 'Argyraeus' (syn. *Epipremnum pictum* 'Argyraeum') Satin potho

36 in. (90 cm) high or more | Warm, minimum 65°F (18°C) | Indirect sunlight

This plant is sold in its juvenile stage, when it has striking large, heart-shaped leaves of a satiny dark olive green with irregular silver spots. In the wild, scindapsus will grow against the trunk of a tree, which offers support as it grows, and this can be replaced indoors with a piece of rough bark or a moss pole. Alternatively, it can trail from a hanging basket.

Caring for plants
Keep moist during spring to autumn, but in winter, apply only sufficient water to prevent the mix from drying out. To maintain high humidity, place the pot on a tray of moist pebbles. Overwatering will cause root rot, and drafts will cause damage to the foliage. Too little light will cause the leaf colors to revert to green. Water with standard liquid fertilizer every 2 weeks in spring to summer.

Making more plants
Take 4-in. (10-cm)-long tip cuttings in spring or early summer, and root in a sterile medium.

Scindapsus pictus 'Argyraeus' (syn. *Epipremnum pictum* 'Argyraeum')

Sedum morganianum
Lamb's tail, Donkey's tail

Stems to
12 in. (30 cm)
high

Normal room
temperature,
cooler in winter

Direct
sunlight

This is an evergreen perennial plant that originates from Mexico. It has numerous floppy, woody-based stems that lie along the soil or trail over the sides of a container. Small, succulent, green-blue leaves cluster around the stems in a spiral arrangement, overlapping each other and curving inward. Small, deep pink flowers are produced in spring and summer if conditions are good. The leaves are easily knocked off this plant, so it should be placed where it is away from accidental damage.

Caring for plants
Keep thoroughly moist during spring to autumn. In winter, apply only sufficient water to prevent the soil mix from drying out. Fertilizing is not necessary.

Making more plants
Take 2–3-in. (5–7.5-cm)-long tip cuttings in spring or summer, and root in a sterile medium.

Sedum morganianum

Selaginella kraussiana
Krauss's spikemoss

2 in.
(5 cm)
high

6 in.
(15 cm)
spread

Cool room
temperature

Indirect
sunlight

This is a mat-forming perennial, which originates from tropical and southern Africa and the Azores. It is grown as a foliage plant and is useful as a low-growing groundcover in a large display, or as a foil to brighter plants in a container. It produces trailing stems clad in finely divided, bright green, mosslike foliage. The creeping stems root as they go, beneath the tiny, scalelike leaves. It produces spores in small terminal spikes.

Caring for plants
Keep moist from spring to autumn, but in winter, apply sufficient water to prevent the soil mix from drying out. Water with standard liquid fertilizer once a month in spring and summer. This plant prefers a slightly acidic soil mix.

Making more plants
Divide mature plants and repot in the spring.

Selaginella kraussiana

Selaginella martensii
Little club moss, Spike moss

12 in.
(30 cm)
high

Normal
room
temperature

Partial
shade

This evergreen, mosslike plant needs constant warm humidity to thrive, so it is ideally suited to use in a bottle garden or terrarium where these conditions can be maintained. It has upright, branching stems bearing tiny bright green leaves and spores, although this is not a fern. Stiff aerial roots grow down from the lower part of the stems to the soil, helping to support the weight of the upper part. *Selaginella martensii* 'Albolineata' is a form in which some leaves are completely or partially white, while *S. martensii* 'Watsoniana' has leaves tipped silver.

Caring for plants
Keep the soil mix thoroughly moist at all times. The foliage is particularly delicate and should never be allowed to dry out, or it will turn brown. Touch it as little as possible and only mist with warm water because cold water will damage it. Water with half-strength liquid fertilizer once a month all year round.

Making more plants
Take 2-in. (5-cm)-long tip cuttings in spring, and root in a sterile medium.

Selaginella martensii

Senecio macroglossus
Natal ivy, Wax vine

| 84 in. (210 cm) high | Normal room temperature. 50–55°F (10–12°C) during the winter rest. | Direct sunlight, indirect sunlight, partial shade |

This is a slender, twining plant bearing a strong resemblance to ivy but with softer, more fleshy, almost succulent-looking leaves. The stems and leaf stalks are purple, and the leaves are mid-green. The form *Senecio macroglossus* 'Variegatus' is most commonly found; it is irregularly marked with cream, some shoots more than others—a few are almost entirely cream-colored. Left to themselves, the stems will trail gracefully, making the plant a good subject for a hanging basket. Alternatively, it can be trained against a frame or thin stakes to give pretty, light-colored height to an arrangement.

Caring for plants
Keep moist during spring to autumn. In winter, apply only sufficient water to prevent the mix from drying out. Water with standard liquid fertilizer every 2 weeks in spring to autumn. The small daisylike flowers will only appear if the plant receives 2–3 hours of direct sunlight every day. If the shade is too deep, the cream variegations will begin to revert to green.

Making more plants
Take 3-in. (7.5-cm)-long tip cuttings in spring or summer, and root in a sterile medium.

Senecio macroglossus

Sinningia speciosa
Gloxinia

8 in.
(20 cm)
high

Normal
room
temperature

Indirect
sunlight,
partial
shade

This is the florist's gloxinia, instantly recognizable by its enormous furry leaves and large bell-shaped flowers. Bought just as the buds begin to open, each plant will provide color for several weeks during the summer, with individual blooms lasting up to a week. Since their introduction during the 19th century, breeding has produced a rich range of flower colors including white, pink, red, maroon, violet, and purple. Varieties include those with a white frill to colored petals, speckles, or splashes of color on a white background, and blooms with a contrasting throat color.

Caring for plants

Keep the soil mix moist at all times while the plant is in leaf. Avoid getting water on the leaves because they will scorch. Water with half-strength tomato fertilizer every 2 weeks, from when flowering stops to when the foliage dies down. The tuber can be stored dry over winter and brought back for a subsequent year by potting up in late winter, hollow side up.

Making more plants

Take cuttings of young leaves and stems in spring or divide larger tubers. Alternatively, sow seed uncovered but mixed with silver sand, in the dark, at 65°F (18°C) in late winter.

Sinningia speciosa

Soleirolia soleirolii

Soleirolia soleirolii
Mind-your-own-business, Baby's tears, Angel's tears, Irish moss

| 2 in. (5 cm) high | Spread limited only by the container | Cool room temperature | Indirect sunlight |

This is a pretty but deceptively quick-growing evergreen perennial plant, which forms a low, creeping mat. It has delicate, intricately branching, almost translucent stems, which root as they spread, and tiny short-stalked bright green leaves. The minute, solitary flowers are borne in the leaf axils. At the front of a mixed arrangement, it is an attractive plant for hiding the container or softening the front edge. *Soleirolia soleirolii.* 'Aurea' has golden green leaves, while *S. soleirolii* 'Variegata' has leaves that are variegated silver. Although this looks like an ideal plant for terrarium, it is actually much too invasive and will swamp the other plants.

Caring for plants
Keep the soil mix moist at all times. Water with half-strength liquid fertilizer every 2 weeks during spring to summer. Trim with scissors to keep it under control in a pot.

Making more plants
Divide rooted clumps of a mature plant.

Soleirolia soleirolii

Solenostemon— Aurora and Kong Series
Coleus

Up to 24 in. (60 cm) high

24 in. (60 cm) spread

Normal room temperature

Indirect sunlight

This subshrub has semisucculent, four-angled stems that are usually upright but sometimes trail. New introductions include the Aurora and Kong series, both of which have more striking leaves than their predecessors. The Aurora series have finely cut leaves in shades of crimson, orange, bronze, yellow, and green. They are more compact than some coleus and form striking specimen plants in their own right. The dramatic leaves on plants in the new Kong series are among the largest available, up to 12 in. (30 cm) long and 8 in. (20 cm) across. They are marked and splashed in shades of green, cream, red, rose, pink, and dark crimson. Both these series of plants are perfect for making a dramatic impact where space allows for a single container.

Caring for plants
Keep the soil mix thoroughly moist throughout the year. Water with standard liquid fertilizer every 2 weeks in spring and summer. The small, mauve flowers should be removed because they are insignificant and draw energy from the leaves.

Making more plants
Take tip cuttings in spring or early summer, and root in a sterile medium.

Top: *Solenostemon*—Aurora series; Bottom: *Solenostemon*—Kong series

Sollya heterophylla
Bluebell creeper, Australian bluebell

| 60 in. (150 cm) high | Cool room temperature | Indirect sunlight |

This is a slender, evergreen, twining climber, with rather weak stems, bearing 1–2-in (2.5–5-cm)-long-oval leaves on short petioles. The leaves are mid- to deep green above and paler beneath. The pretty, nodding, bell-like blue flowers are produced in summer and autumn, in clusters of 4–12. Each is slender-stalked, with 5 petals measuring ½ in. (12 mm) long. It is found naturally in light woodland and is hardy outdoors in mild areas, although where these conditions cannot be guaranteed, it is an attractive subject for a cool, but well-lit greenhouse.

Caring for plants
Keep the soil mix moist during spring to autumn. In winter, water sparingly. Water with standard liquid fertilizer once a month in spring to autumn. Avoid pinching the shoots because the flowers are borne at the tips and will be removed.

Making more plants
Sow seed in spring, or take 4-in. (10-cm)-long tip cuttings in late spring or summer. Root it in a sterile medium.

Sollya heterophylla

Sparmannia africana
African hemp

84 in. (210 cm) high   Normal to cool room temperature   Indirect sunlight

This is a quick-growing treelike shrub, with large, evergreen, downy leaves of a pale apple green up to 9 in. (23 cm) long. The flowers are borne in long-stalked clusters and can appear all year round if the conditions are right. Each is white and 4-petaled, drooping down in bud, then straightening up as it opens to reveal purple-tipped golden yellow stamens. This is an ideal plant for a greenhouse or cool porch, where it has the room to grow and flourish. *Sparmannia africana* 'Flore Pleno' is a form with double flowers, while S. *africana* 'Variegata' has leaves marked with white.

Caring for plants
Keep thoroughly moist during spring to autumn. In winter, apply only sufficient water to prevent the compost from drying out. Water with standard liquid fertilizer every 2 weeks from spring to autumn. Pinch out shoot tips regularly to encourage bushing.

Making more plants
Take 6-in. (15-cm)-long tip cuttings in spring, and root in soil mix or water. This plant grows so quickly and roots so readily from cuttings that it is worth replacing the parent every 2–3 years and discarding it.

Sparmannia africana

Spathiphyllum wallisii

Spathiphyllum wallisii
Peace lily

36 in.
(90 cm)
high

Normal
room
temperature

Indirect
sunlight

This is a stemless plant, with glossy dark green leaves up to 14 in. (35 cm) long and 4 in. (10 cm) wide on petioles of up to 8 in. (20 cm), which grow directly from the rhizome. The striking arumlike flowers are produced on stalks up to 12 in. (30 cm) long and consist of a concave, oval spathe that starts off white and gradually changes to green, surrounding a white, scented spadix.

Caring for plants
Keep moist at all times. Water with standard liquid fertilizer every 2 weeks from spring to autumn. Dry air should be avoided at all times by setting the pot on a tray of moist pebbles. In warm conditions, the plant will not have a definite rest period, and both watering and fertilizing should be reduced but continued.

Making more plants
Divide mature plants in spring, and plant each part in potting soil in individual pots.

Stephanotis floribunda
Madagascar jasmine, Wax flower

10 ft. (3 m) high or more

Normal to warm room temperature

Indirect sunlight

This climbing shrub is best known for its heavily scented, waxy white flowers, but it also has wonderful leathery leaves of a glossy dark green. The 1¼-in. (3-cm)-long flowers are produced in clusters of 10 or more, each being tubular in shape, flaring out into 5 lobes. It needs support as it grows, but this plant will look equally attractive in a greenhouse, trained against a wall, or indoors on a small trellis or over an archway, as long as it is positioned where its fragrance can be fully appreciated.

Caring for plants

Keep thoroughly moist from spring to autumn. In winter, apply only sufficient water to prevent the soil mix drying out. Set in a tray of pebbles to increase humidity, and mist daily if the temperature rises. Water with standard liquid fertilizer every 2 weeks in spring to summer. Pinch growing tips to encourage bushy growth.

Making more plants

Take tip cuttings, and root in a sterile medium.

Stephanotis floribunda

Streptocarpus x *hybridus*
Cape primrose

12 in.
(30 cm)
high

18 in.
(47 cm)
spread

Normal
room
temperature

Indirect
sunlight

Many *Streptocarpus* hybrids have been bred, but the ones usually seen as indoor plants tend to be 'Constant Nymph' or 'John Innes'. These have a rosette of coarse, primroselike leaves arising directly from the base of the plant, and from these, the flower stalks are produced, bearing single or multiple blooms in shades of purple, blue, mauve, red, pink, or white, according to the variety. The flowers may be followed by interesting, twisted seed pods, but these should be removed to promote further flowering. *Streptocarpus* x *hybridus* 'Constant Nymph' has pale blue-mauve flowers, with darker lines in the throat, while S. x *hybridus* 'John Innes' has flowers that range from pale pink to blue and purple.

Caring for plants
Allow to dry slightly between waterings. Keep away from drafts and cold air, and increase humidity, particularly in high temperatures, by misting. Water with half-strength high-potash liquid fertilizer every 2 weeks from spring to autumn.

Making more plants
Take leaf cuttings in spring, divide mature plants, or sow seed in spring.

Streptocarpus x *hybridus*

Syngonium podophyllum
Arrowhead plant,
Goosefoot plant

84 in.
(210 cm)
high

Normal
room
temperature

Indirect
sunlight

The young leaves of the syngonium are shaped like arrowheads, and are leathery, glossy, and brightly colored. As the plant ages, long stems grow, which can either be trailed from a hanging basket or trained up a support. These bear the mature leaves, which are progressively three- and then five-lobed. Cutting off the long stems as they develop will prolong the juvenile stage with its attractive foliage. S. *podophyllum* 'Emerald Gem' has leaves that are fleshy and shiny dark green, S. *podophyllum* 'Silver Knight' has silver-green leaves, and S. *podophyllum* 'Variegatum' has leaves splashed with pale green. Syngonium is an ideal subject for growing up a moss pole because it has aerial roots.

Caring for plants
Keep moist during spring to autumn. In winter, apply only sufficient water to prevent the soil mix from drying out. Mist regularly, especially in high temperatures to prevent the foliage from drying out. Water with standard liquid fertilizer every 2 weeks from spring to summer.

Making more plants
Take 4-in. (10-cm)-long tip cuttings in spring, or stem cuttings with aerial roots in spring or summer. Root in a sterile medium.

Syngonium podophyllum

Thunbergia alata
Black-eyed Susan

84 in.
(210 cm)
high

Cool to
normal room
temperature

Some direct
sunlight daily
is essential to
good flowering

This is a reliable, quick-growing, twining plant, normally grown as an annual, which gives a colorful display of flowers throughout the summer and will easily cover a screen or trellis. The toothed leaves are triangular in shape, surrounding flowers that are trumpet-shaped and up to 2 in. (5 cm) across in shades of orange, yellow, or white, each with a chocolate brown eye. Several plants can be grown together in a container on a tepee of canes to give an impressive splash of color in a sunroom. Single plants can be grown up strings in a window or allowed to trail gracefully from a hanging basket.

Caring for plants
Keep the soil mix thoroughly moist. Water with standard liquid fertilizer every 2 weeks. Pinch the flowers as they fade to ensure the production of more.

Making more plants
Sow seed in germinating mix in spring.

Thunbergia alata

Thymus x *citriodorus*
Lemon-scented thyme

12 in. (30 cm) high

Warm room temperature of 60–70ºF (15–21ºC)

At least 6 hours of direct sunlight every day

This forms a twiggy, round shrub up to 12 in. (30 cm) high with masses of small oval leaves. Upright heads of pale pink flowers appear in summer. A strong scent of lemon is released if the leaves are crushed. The fresh or dried leaves are sometimes used in cooking, particularly in fish dishes, but the flavor can be quite strong. Thymus needs several hours of sunshine each day, so chose a sunny windowsill for it to sit on. It is also often grown in the herb garden, but it should be in containers that can be moved to shelter because the plant will go dormant in low temperatures.

Caring for plants

Water sparingly but regularly and do not allow the soil mix to become too wet. Water with standard liquid fertilizer every 2 weeks in spring, once a month in summer. Turn the plants daily to prevent their becoming one-sided. Keep them in as draft-free a position as possible, although they do enjoy fresh air daily.

Making more plants

Sow seed in spring, and plant the seedlings in individual pots as soon as they are large enough to handle. Alternatively, take 2-in. (5-cm)-long tip cuttings in summer before flowering starts.

Thymus x *citriodorus*

Thymus vulgaris
Thyme

| 12 in. (30 cm) high | Warm room temperature of 60–70°F (15–21°C) | At least 6 hours of direct sunlight every day |

This is a hardy, evergreen subshrub with tiny fragrant leaves. Leaves can be picked and used at any time, or they can be dried and stored to be used in stuffings, soups, sauces, and meat dishes, although the flavor can be quite strong. Thymus needs several hours of sunshine each day, so choose a sunny windowsill for it to sit on. It is also quite often grown in the herb garden, but it should be in containers that can be moved to shelter because the plant will go dormant in low temperatures.

Caring for plants

Keep the soil mix moist at all times. Water with standard liquid fertilizer every 2 weeks in spring, once a month in summer. Turn the plants daily to prevent their becoming one-sided. Keep them in as draft-free a position as possible—but they enjoy fresh air daily.

Making more plants

Sow seed in spring and plant the seedlings in individual pots as soon as they are large enough to handle. Alternatively, layer the stem or take 2-in. (5-cm)-long tip cuttings in spring.

Thymus vulgaris

Tibouchina urvilleana
Brazilian spider flower

72 in. (180 cm) high   36 in. (90 cm) spread   Cool room temperature   Indirect sunlight

This is a handsome shrub that originates from Brazil. It has an erect-to-spreading habit and squarish stems covered in a layer of fine reddish hairs. The leaves are around 3 in. (7.5 cm) long, oval to elliptical in shape, mid- to dark green in color, and covered with a layer of fine velvetlike hair. Glowing reddish purple flowers with dark, hooked stamens are carried in clusters from summer well into the autumn. These flowers are up to 4 in. (10 cm) across and have a satinlike texture when touched.

Caring for plants
Keep moist from spring to autumn. In winter, apply sufficient water to prevent the soil mix from drying out. Water with standard liquid fertilizer once a month in spring and summer. Prune in late winter to restrict growth.

Making more plants
Take semiripe cuttings in summer, and root in a sterile medium.

Tibouchina urvilleana

Tillandsia lindenii
Blue-flowered torch

33 in.
(80 cm)
high

Warm
(above
60°F/15°C)

Indirect
sunlight

The smooth, arching leaves of tillandsia are dark green above and purple below, arranged in a loose rosette, and are up to 18 in. (47 cm) in length. The flower spike grows to around 15 in. (40 cm) high and consists of a hard, long-lasting head 9–12 in. (23–30 cm) long, made up of numerous densely overlapping, rose-pink bracts. From between the bracts, the true flowers emerge singly, each up to 3 in. (7.5 cm) long, with a rich shade of royal blue and a white throat.

Caring for plants
Because the roots serve little purpose in gathering moisture for the plant, the plant should be thoroughly mist-sprayed 2 or 3 times a week. The water that runs off should be adequate to supply the soil mix. High humidity is essential, so set the plant on a tray of moist pebbles. Water with half-strength liquid fertilizer once a month, applied in the spray.

Making more plants
Take 3-in. (7.5-cm)-long offsets at any time, severing them from the parent plant with a sharp knife. Rooting should take 4–6 months.

Tillandsia lindenii

Tolmiea menziesii
Pickaback plant,
Mother of thousands

12 in.
(30 cm)
high

Cool to
normal
room
temperature

Any except
intense midday
sun or deep
shade

The common name of this plant is derived from the way in which the young plants develop on the older leaves at the point where the leaf joins the petiole. The weight of these new plants pulls the leaves down so that they have a trailing appearance, which looks attractive when the plant is in a hanging basket. The foliage is lime green and covered with fine hairs, giving it a downy appearance. Small greenish white flowers are produced in late-spring to early summer.

Caring for plants

Keep moist in spring to autumn. In winter, apply only sufficient water to prevent the soil mix from drying out. Water with standard liquid fertilizer every 2 weeks during spring to summer. If a tolmiea outgrows its allotted space, it can be planted outdoors and replaced indoors by a young plantlet.

Making more plants

Use well-developed plantlets, and either peg them down into a pot of soil mix or detach and push the petiole into the mix to keep the leaf in good contact with it.

Other varieties

Tolmeia menziesii 'Taff's Gold' is a clump-forming perennial with a creeping, spreading habit. The plant forms a web of horizontal stems. The maplelike leaves are about 5 in. (12.5 cm) long, with toothed margins, and are pale green in color with a mottling of pale yellow and cream flecks and covered in a layer of fine, spiky hairs.

Tolmiea menziesii

Trachelospermum jasminoides
Star jasmine

10 ft.
(3 m)
high

Cool room
temperature

Full sun to
partial
shade

This is a woody, evergreen climber, with oval-shaped, dark green, glossy leaves, about 4 in. (10 cm) long and green twining stems that turn brown and woody with age. As these stems age, they often produce aerial, clinging roots at regular intervals. The foliage may turn bronze in low temperatures. From mid- to late summer, fragrant, 1 in. (2.5 cm) wide, pure white tubular flowers, which open into a star shape, are produced in small clusters on the shoot tips and along the branches.

Caring for plants
Water freely from spring until autumn; then apply only enough water to prevent the soil mix from drying out. Water with a balanced liquid fertilizer every 4 weeks in spring and summer.

Making more plants
Take semiripe cuttings in summer, and root in a sterile medium.

Trachelospermum jasminoides

Tradescantia fluminensis
T. albiflora 'Albovittata'
Spider-lily, Wandering Jew,
Inch plant

Stems to 18 in. (47 cm) long   Normal room temperature   Some direct sunlight daily to maintain leaf color

The stems of tradescantia will trail profusely from a shelf or hanging basket, each turning upward at its lower end. The leaves have a translucent appearance and arise directly from the succulent-looking stems, causing it to change direction slightly at each joint. Small white or pale pink, 3-petaled flowers are produced in spring and summer in clusters on short stalks. *Tradescantia fluminensis* 'Albovittata' has leaves that are white-striped, *T. fluminensis* 'Aurea' has yellow leaves, *T. fluminensis* 'Laekenensis' has small leaves that are pale green striped and banded with white tinted purple, and *T. fluminensis* 'Quicksilver' is quick growing and has green-and-white-striped leaves.

Caring for plants
Keep the soil mix thoroughly moist in spring to autumn, and drier in winter. Water with standard liquid fertilizer every 2 weeks during spring to autumn. Pinch out tips regularly to encourage a bushy plant.

Making more plants
Take 4-in. (10-cm)-long tip cuttings in spring to autumn, and root in water or potting soil.

Tradescantia albiflora 'Albovittata'

Tradescantia spathacea (*was Rhoeo discolor*)
Oyster plant, Cradle lily, Moses in the bulrushes

18 in. (47 cm) high   Normal room temperature   Indirect sunlight

The common names of this plant arise from the unusual arrangement of the flower bracts, which are paired in the shape of a boat, with the small white, 3-petaled flowers in the middle. These are set amid a loose rosette of lance-shaped, semisucculent leaves, which are dark green or dark blue-green above, purple beneath, and set atop a short, stout stem. *Tradescantia spathacea* 'Vittata' ('Variegata') has leaves striped cream above and deep purple beneath.

Caring for plants
Keep the soil mix moist in spring to autumn and drier in winter. These plants cannot tolerate dry air or drafts, so set on a tray of moist pebbles. Water with standard liquid fertilizer every 2 weeks during spring to summer.

Making more plants
Take offsets from the base of the plant after flowering, and plant in individual small pots.

Tradescantia spathacea

Tulipa
Tulip

Variable

Cool,
60–65°F
(16–18°C)

Indirect
sunlight

Tulips are not as easy as some of the other bulbs to grow indoors, but they are well worth attempting. Choose varieties that are labeled for indoor growing, such as forms of *Tulipa greigii* or *T. kaufmanniana*, as these are less likely to be affected by the warmer conditions and become drawn and weak. Both have a range of flower colors, with both plain and striped petals, and both have attractively marked foliage.

Recommended varieties are *T. kaufmanniana* 'Giuseppe Verdi', which is 6–12 in. (15–30 cm) high with yellow-and-red-striped flowers, and *T. greigii* 'Red Riding Hood', which has red flowers.

Caring for plants
Keep the soil mix moist at all times while the plant is in flower, until the leaves turn yellow. Fertilizing is not necessary.

Making more plants
Remove offsets from dormant bulbs, and transplant individually.

Other varieties
T. praestans 'Unicum' produces red blooms with yellow bases and dark blue–black anthers. Each flower is 4–5 in. (10–12.5 cm) across when fully open. This plant is quite hardy and can be planted outdoors after the display or allowed to die down naturally in the container and kept for another year. Feed at weekly intervals for 3–4 weeks after flowering.

Tulipa

Vriesia splendens
Flaming sword

Up to 39 in.
(100 cm)
high
in flower

Normal
room
temperature

Direct
sunlight
except
midday
in summer

Vriesia is one of the bromeliads that is grown for both its flowers and its foliage. The leaves measure 15 in. (40 cm) in length and are dark green with broad, dark purple-brown crossbands. The flower spike grows to about 24 in. (60 cm) in height and consists of a flattened, blade-shaped head of tightly compressed, bright scarlet bracts, each up to 3 in. (7.5 cm) long. The yellow flowers emerge from between the bracts and measure about 2 in. (5 cm) long. They are fairly short-lived, but the hard flower head and colored bracts persist for several weeks.

Caring for plants
Keep the central cup filled with water at all times. Water with half-strength liquid fertilizer once a month into both the cup and potting soil.

Making more plants
Using a sharp knife, detach 3–6 in. (7.5–15 cm) long offsets from the base of the plant, not from the leaf axils. Pot singly and enclose in a plastic bag. Rooting should take about 6 weeks. After it has flowered, each rosette dies, so make sure when taking material for propagation that a replacement for the parent plant is left.

Vriesia splendens

Yucca filamentosa
Spoonleaf yucca, Adam's needle, Needle palm

60 in.
(150 cm)
high

Normal
room
temperature

Direct
sunlight

The typical yucca plant has a stout, woody stem and stiff, sword-shaped leaves arranged in loose rosettes at the tips of each branch. The edges of the leaves have long, thin threadlike hairs hanging from them. Although it is slow-growing, it is capable of reaching a height of 60 in. (150 cm) and looks best where it has room to develop to the full, such as in a cool greenhouse or hallway. *Yucca filamentosa* 'Bright Edge' grows to 24 in. (60 cm) and has leaves broadly edged in butter yellow. *Y. filamentosa* 'Variegata' has leaves edged white, which become pink-tinted.

Caring for plants
Keep thoroughly moist in spring to autumn. In winter, apply only sufficient water to prevent the soil mix from drying out. Feed with standard liquid fertilizer every 2 weeks during spring to autumn. The plant can be placed outdoors during the summer months, in a location that receives some direct sunlight every day.

Making more plants
Take cane cuttings or offsets, and root in a sterile medium.

Yucca filamentosa

Zantedeschia aethiopica

Zantedeschia aethiopica
Arum lily, Calla lily

36 in.
(90 cm)
high

Cool to
normal
room
temperature

Direct
sunlight

This is a rhizomatous plant with long, glossy, deep green leaves shaped like arrowheads. The flower head consists of a large, milk white spathe that curls back to reveal a golden yellow spadix on a stalk up to 18 in. (47 cm) long. Zantedeschias are hardy outdoors in many areas where flowering occurs during the spring, followed by a natural rest period. Indoor plants need to follow the same pattern—after flowering, the plant needs to be placed in a cool spot, preferably outdoors, for the foliage to die down. If the zantedeschia is planted outdoors permanently after flowering, it will need a marshy or wet position.

Caring for plants
Keep moist as the plants come into leaf and again as they die down after flowering. However, while they are in full flower, they need to be wet and can actually stand in water. Water with standard liquid fertilizer every 2 weeks from when the plant is in full leaf until the end of the flowering season.

Making more plants
Divide mature plants in autumn.

Glossary

adventitious A root that forms in an unusual location, such as high on the stem.

aerial roots Roots that emerge from the stem above soil level; they often cling to trees and other supports.

aerate Loosening or puncturing the soil to increase water penetration.

aerole A cushionlike raised or depressed area bearing spines, hairs, or flowers in cacti.

air layering A specialized method of plant propagation accomplished by cutting into the bark of the plant to induce new roots to form.

annuals Plants whose life cycle lasts only one growing season, from seed to blooms to seed.

anther Pollen-producing part of the flower, often carried on a long filament.

axil The angle between the stem and the leaf or leafstalk growing from it.

biennial A plant that usually only lives two years, normally producing flowers and seed the second year.

bract A modified leaf at the base of a flower or flower head, which can look like a leaf or a petal and can be brightly colored.

bulbil Small, immature bulb formed at the base of mature bulbs or in the axil of a leaf, bract, or sometimes, flower head.

calyx The outermost part of a flower consisting of separate or joined sepals.

capillary matting Porous material that retains liquid. Capillary describes the action of a substance drawing water through the matting when the matting is in contact with water.

corolla The petals or primary decorative feature of a flower.

cultivar (abbreviated cv.) Usually a variety raised in cultivation, rather than occurring in the wild. Cultivar plant names tend to be in a modern language instead of Latin, enclosed within single quote marks.

division Method of propagation that involves splitting a plant into two or more parts, each with its own roots and leaves.

double Describes a flower with at least two full layers of petals.

epiphyte A plant that naturally grows on the body of another plant, or sometimes on rocks, but feeds independently.

F1 hybrid First generation offspring from two distinct parents.

glochid A small, barbed bristle or hair arising from the areole of a cactus.

heel Strip of bark and wood torn from the lower part of a main stem when a sideshoot is pulled downward.

heel cutting A short, side branch taken as a cutting with a small piece of the main stem (often taken with old rose cuttings).

honeydew The sticky secretion produced by sucking insects such as aphids.

hybrid The natural or artificially produced offspring of genetically different parents belonging to the same family.

hydroculture Growing plants without soil but in sand, Vermiculite or other granular material, using a liquid solution of nutrients to feed them.

interspecific hybrid A cross between two species of the same genus.

layering Means of propagation that pegs a stem to the soil while still attached to the parent plant so it will root separately.

leaf node The point on a stem where leaves and shoots arise.

offsets Small plants that develop naturally at the bases of mature plants, especially bulbous plants.

palmate Describes a leaf with three or more leaflets or lobes coming from a single point on a leafstalk; literally means hand-shaped.

peduncle The stalk of a flower.

perennial A plant that lives for three seasons—or more—usually indefinitely.

perlite Expanded volcanic rock.

pest Any insect or animal that is detrimental to the health and well-being of plants.

petiole Another term for leafstalk.

photosynthesis The process by which plants convert carbon dioxide into starches and sugars.

phototropism When a plant receives light from

one direction only and grows toward it, resulting in lopsidedness.

pinching out The process of removing the soft growing tips of a plant with the fingers to encourage bushy growth.

pinna/pinnae Leaflet(s) of pinnate leaf or fern frond, resembling a smaller leaf in its own right.

plantlet A young, small plant that develops naturally on an older plant.

pot-bound A plant whose root system has outgrown its pot.

pricking out Moving seedlings from the pots in which they were sown to plant them individually or farther apart in new containers.

propagation The means by which the plants increase or are increased.

pseudobulb A swollen bulblike stem.

pseudostem A stemlike structure composed of tightly packed leaf bases.

raceme A group of flowers on a stalk with the youngest at the tip.

rachis The main stalk of a compound leaf or flower.

rhizome Fleshy stem, usually horizontal and growing underground, which often acts as a storage system.

rooting hormone A powder or liquid growth hormone used to promote the development of roots on a cutting.

semi-double Describes a flower with two or three times the number of petals of a single flower, usually in two or three layers.

semiripe cutting A cutting taken from a woody stem that is half ripened.

sepal A part of the calyx, which is sometimes colorful and petal-like, but usually green and smaller than the petals.

single A flower with one layer of petals.

spadix A special type of fleshy flower spike, usually embedded with tiny, stalk-less flowers, which often sits within a spathe.

spathe Modified leaf or hoodlike bract that surrounds the spadix.

sphagnum A bog moss that is collected and composted. This moss is also packaged and sold fresh, and used for lining hanging baskets and air layering.

sporangium A spore-producing organ on the underside of a fern leaf.

spore A reproductive unit of many nonflowering plants.

stamen The male, pollen bearing part of a flower, usually comprised of an anther carried on filament.

stigma The tip of the female flower organ, which receives pollen.

stolon An arching horizontal or trailing stem that roots and produces new shoots at its tips.

stoloniferous A plant that spreads by means of arching horizontal or trailing stems.

sucker Growth originating from the rootstock of a grafted plant, rather than the desired part of the plant. Sucker growth should be removed, so it doesn't draw energy from the plant.

tender plants Plants that are unable to endure frost or freezing temperatures.

tendril The twisting, clinging, slender growth on many vines, which allows the plant to attach itself to a support or trellis.

transpiration The loss of water via a plant's leaves.

tubercles A small, wart-like projection.

Vermiculite The mineral "mica," which has been heated to the point of expansion. A good addition to container potting mixes, Vermiculite retains moisture and air within the soil.

Index

Picture credits

All photographs copyright of Collins & Brown except the following:

Ray Cox Photography: page 275

Garden World Images: pages 54, 112

Garden Matters: pages 53, 124, 179, 186, 190, 230

John Glover: pages 111, 270